Plants: Answers That Work

Ann

July 1979

Plants:
Answers That Work

Ken Reeves

Clarke, Irwin & Company Limited
Toronto/Vancouver

Line illustrations by Deborah Drew-Brook

Canadian Cataloguing in Publication Data

Reeves, Ken, 1923-
   Plants: answers that work

Includes index.
ISBN 0-7720-1214-8 pa.

1. House plants. I. Title.

SB419.R43   635.9'65   C78-001407-3

Printed in Canada

This book is dedicated to all our customers and to the listeners of CBC Toronto's Radio Noon who have honoured me with their questions on plants and gardens.

Acknowledgements

I gratefully acknowledge the plant scientists and university and government extension agents of Canada and the United States who devote their lives to the research and dissemination of knowledge that makes horticulture more fruitful and rewarding.

Contents

Introduction

I have great empathy with the novice gardener. Although I grew up in greenhouses and on a market garden, it was my older brother Frank who had the green thumb in my generation. I was more mechanically inclined. Even horses, the source of power around the market garden, did not interest me that much. Turning a bushel-footed crossbred Clydesdale around on a headland (at an age when I had to reach up to the scuffler handles) required all my strength and usually took out at least six cabbages.

As I balanced the scuffler down between the rows, placing bare feet carefully on the cool, moist furrows of the scuffler teeth, i dreamed of tractors. There were obvious incentives to these fantasies. Walking behind a horse on a hot July day flares the nostrils and necessitates some fancy footwork, too.

Enlistment in the R.C.A.F. on my eighteenth birthday marked the pursuit of another dream—to be a pilot. Although I was a moderate success at this, I discovered that the military world was not the place I wanted to spend a lifetime. And so, after the Second World War, I entered the School of Empirical Horticulture, from which I have never graduated. When you read later on in this book that "light is the thing that makes everything happen," know that I found this out the hard way. We were just beginning to apply the knowledge that Chrysanthemums flower in response to shortened day length. We achieved this by building a crude, light framework over the greenhouse benches of Mums, covering the plants with opaque black cloth late every afternoon and removing it in the morning. A few varieties just weren't responding, so I decided to intensify the treatment by having the black cloth over the errant cultivars night and day for a whole week. The foliage rapidly faded to a yellowish green and all growth came to a halt. Ergo: plants need light every day to grow.

While I did take botany in grade nine, it was really one of my nobler experiments with Geraniums that taught me the important function of leaves on a plant. We had just taken a batch of tip cuttings off our big, healthy stock plants of Geraniums. I knew that any subsequent cuttings would have to come from below the densely packed leaves that remained on the stock plants. Since I reasoned that light had to reach down below these leaves to where the leaf petioles joined the main stem of the plant, why not strip off all the leaves and give those embryo cuttings full benefit of the available light?

This I did on a large block of stock plants. The long, fat stems stood naked above the pots like corn stalks after a hail storm. As days went by and little or no new growth appeared, my gleeful anticipation of increased cutting production faded. A visiting plant scientist explained that when I had removed all the leaves, I had removed the "factory" that causes plants to grow.

There has never been a lack of problems and questions as consumer interest focuses more and more on growing plants and flowers. Early in our experience of retailing plant material, we realized that if our enterprise was to succeed, our customers had to be successful in growing the plants they bought. We had to provide the information and products that ensured results, and diagnose the problems that prevented success. Our sales area became a forum for promoting new and better products, and a place where people could ask questions.

These daily experiences were given a broader audience with what was initially intended to be a single appearance on a live phone-in program over CBC radio in Toronto. A former CBC employee, Joanne Silverman, was working as our Public Relations Officer, and heard that John Barberash, producer of Radio Noon, was looking for an expert to answer "gardening" questions. Any contacts he had that were eligible to do the job were either not available or wanted only prepared questions and answers.

I came away from an interview with John and Diana Baillie, his assistant, with grave misgivings. I felt that my experience in many areas of horticulture was shallow or non-existent. I had pretty well decided to decline when Joanne leaked the proposal to my family. Where was that Roll-Em-Again-Ken spirit that rose to any challenge, they wanted to know. So I found myself sitting opposite David Schatzky, the host of Radio Noon at that time, in the old Parliament Street studio, waiting for the news to end and the first phone hook up to a questioner. A situation like that surely improves one's prayer life.

From the first broadcast, the four phone lines filled with questioners and blinked silently on hold. We have not run out of questions since. Recently we did a broadcast from the Spring Flower Show in Toronto. The added dimension of being able to see the audience and questioners was extra fun. However, on a regular program from the studio, the producer turns away callers when the time is up. At the Flower Show they simply lined up after the allotted air time and the questions kept coming for another hour. There were even questions waiting when I returned to our booth. No longer was I the voice without a face. Finally, I slipped away to a quiet chair in the mezzanine overlooking the Show, propped my head up in one hand and fell sound asleep. About half an hour later, as my eyes were just blinking awake, a woman sitting on a chair right beside me said, "Mr. Reeves, I have a question I would like to ask you. My plant is . . . "

Often the questions are preceded by the questioners' self-assessment of their inability to "grow anything." Take heart. If, by the grace of God, this greasy-thumbed, would-be engineer can become a green-thumbed plant expert, then there is hope for everyone.

Ken Reeves

Chapter 1
Potting

When to Repot

I would like to ask about a Schefflera that a friend of mine received as a wedding gift three months ago. Now she says that she can see roots right on the surface of the soil and she told me that because of this she is going to repot it. I just about had a fit. It shouldn't have to be repotted in just three months, should it?

Is it growing actively?

Yes. It's practically one and a half metres high.

It is amazing how large a Schefflera you can have in a 30 or 35 cm pot. They can be one to two metres high. The fact that there are roots on the surface is not an indication that it needs repotting. It just means that the plant has a healthy root system. But the larger the plant and the smaller the pot and soil ball, the more frequently you are going to have to water. The real issue, I believe, is whether or not the plant looks out of bounds and tippy in the pot. If it still looks in balance, then you can leave it there. However, I would check to see how your friend is watering the plant. If she is just keeping the surface of the soil wet then the roots, of course, are going to stay on the surface.

No, she says she is watering it so that the water runs right through the pot.

I don't think that you have a problem then as long as the plant is pleasing to the eye. When the Schefflera grows larger and looks out of balance in its present pot, simply place the plant in a container one or two sizes larger, putting porous potting soil around the old root ball. You can plant a Schefflera down deeper than it was in its old pot. The plant will simply root out of the stem that has been buried, and sometimes you can cover up some unattractive stem in this manner. It also helps the plant to root out into the new media around it if you scarify the old roots by scratching them with a heavy fork, pulling them away from the root ball.

Selecting the right pot size for any given plant is as much a matter of aesthetics as it is a cultural necessity. Generally speaking, what is pleasing to the eye determines the correct pot size for that plant. With an indoor plant, it is amazing how large a plant can thrive in a rather small pot. If you select a pot which is oversized for the plant, the possibility of overwatering is much greater than if the pot size is matched correctly to the plant. If there is an excess volume of soil and hence an excess reservoir of water relative to the size of the plant, drying out of the soil will take place very slowly. Drying out is essential to draw fresh supplies of oxygen into the spaces occupied by the water. An oxygen supply at the roots is essential to survival and growth. Potted plants outdoors subjected to higher light and greater air movement will transpire water more quickly, making overwatering less likely, and necessitating very frequent watering on undersized pots.

When a plant becomes tippy because the pot is too small, or when you have to water very frequently (every other day) because the soil

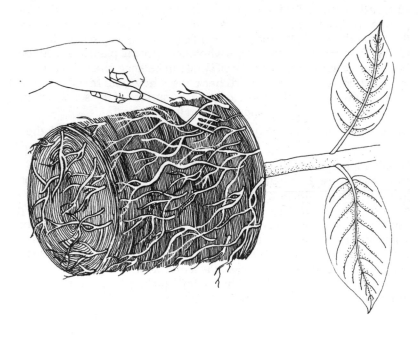

To redirect old roots into the new soil after repotting, scarify about half of the roots by prying them loose from the root ball. Do not be concerned about breaking some of them; this encourages the roots to branch out in the same way as pruning the top of the plant usually results in new branches.

volume is so small in relation to the size of the plant, or when the ratio of the pot size to plant size is no longer pleasing to the eye, then this is the time to increase the size of the pot. Another consideration is the

As much as twenty-five per cent of the outer diameter of a root-bound root ball may be sliced off if an established plant needs repotting back into the same pot. Replace the discarded roots and root ball with new potting soil. If the plant lends itself to pruning, this should also be done. If it does not, mist the plant and cover it with a clear plastic bag for two to three weeks until new roots develop to support the water requirements of the leaves. Mist frequently enough to keep the leaves from wilting.

length of time that the plant has been in the pot. If the plant has been growing in the pot a year or two, it may have developed a very large root system. When the roots fill in the air spaces in the soil, root rot problems can occur. In such cases, it might be wise to up-pot into a porous soil with more oxygen-holding capacity and scarify the roots to encourage them to establish new root growing patterns. But do not remove the old soil unless there have been serious drainage problems. New open soil all around the old root ball will often correct stubborn drainage problems.

A plant may not be thriving because it has become root bound growing in the same container for two years or more. Yet you cannot put it in a larger pot because it must fit a decorative container or you simply do not want a larger container. If the shape and type of plant lends itself to cutting back the top growth then you can also cut back the roots. Repot into the same container with fresh potting soil. Misting and covering with clear plastic may be necessary for a week or two until new roots are evident by the appearance of new growth on top. This operation is best done in a season of high light.

Repotting a plant is seldom recommended, if, by repotting, we mean that we take the plant out of the pot, shake off all the soil and put it into a pot in new soil. This process removes from a third to three quarters of the root system of the plant and puts it into deep shock. The real working parts of the root system are the fine roots which are the first to be lost in a repotting operation accompanied by soil removal.

This drastic operation might be necessary, however, when the existing soil has such poor drainage that it is impossible for water to run through, or when it runs through so slowly that the soil never dries out. In this case, the oxygen supply in the soil is so poor that growth rate is badly affected, and foliage begins to yellow and fall off. Under these circumstances you may have to actually take the plant out of the pot, remove that soil and put it in well-drained soil.

Soil removal might also be required if, because of high salts or improper watering, most of the root system is rotting. This makes the roots highly vulnerable to disease organisms. In this case it would be best to remove the plant carefully from the soil and wash the root system to try to remove the portions that have rotted. Then repot it in sterilized, open potting soil.

If repotting is necessary because of the reasons outlined above, keep in mind that you must now propagate new roots on the plant. The roots that remain are probably simply carrier roots that bring the moisture and fertilizer up into the plant. New fine feeder roots will have to be propagated. In the meantime you should mist the leaves of the plant and consider putting it under a plastic bag to keep the humidity up and stop excessive transpiration and wilting. A thorough drenching of the soil with a spray dilution strength of benomyl fungicide is also a good idea if there has been root damage.

Potting Soils

I would like to pot some new plants. Can I use ordinary garden soil for this?

One of the keys to successful plants is the potting soil you use. It should be at least twenty per cent air to provide the essential oxygen for the functioning of the roots. This porous structure must also allow water to pass down from the surface, and any surplus must quickly find its way out the drainage holes. The soil must be able to absorb plant nutrients and release them to the plant's root system as required. It must also be free of soil-borne diseases.

You can almost never meet these requirements by using even the best of garden soils as the sole ingredient of a potting soil. The root system of a plant growing unrestricted in a good garden soil is much larger than that of a pot-grown plant. While the air spaces of the denser garden soil are much smaller, the root system can reach out into a greater volume of soil, finding sufficient air, moisture and the nutrients required. Potting soil should have coarse ingredients with a greater air reservoir capacity by volume. The porous structure provides larger channels to conduct water quickly through the mix and out the drainage holes, pulling air into the potting mix from the surface as it drains away.

A garden soil that produces good crops of vegetables or flowers can be used in a potting soil if adapted to give the necessary porosity and drainage. It must be soil that you can cultivate in your garden twenty-four hours after a heavy rain without it being sticky. It should also be just as readily cultivated after a long dry spell without your tools bouncing off the surface. If your garden soil doesn't meet these minimum requirements then it will not benefit any potting mixture even in small quantities.

The most effective and readily available agents to convert garden soil into potting soil are fine to medium shredded sphagnum moss and one of numbers 2, 3, or 4 horticultural vermiculite or perlite, or coarse concrete-grade sand (brick sand is too fine). The initial mix can be three equal parts by volume. After thoroughly mixing, check the drainage by filling a pot with the soil up to within 2 cm of the rim of the pot. Then flood the soil with water, filling the pot right to the rim. It should only take about forty-five seconds for that water to soak down and out through the drainage hole. If the drainage is slow then decrease the amount of garden soil and increase the other two ingredients until the final mix drains properly.

While peat, perlite and vermiculite can be considered disease and weed free, soil and sand cannot. The resultant mix can be sterilized by filling cake pans level full and placing them in a 105°C oven. Using a meat thermometer, raise the temperature of the mix to 80°C for thirty minutes. Over 100°C and/or longer than thirty minutes can cause chemical changes in the soil that kill beneficial soil bacteria. Under 60°C and/or less than twenty minutes will not kill some disease pathogens and weed seeds.

Unfortunately, buying prepared potting soil does not ensure that you have a mix in which your plants will thrive. I have seen packaged potting soils that were almost impervious to water. Try to buy your potting soil from greenhouses where they retail the same soil that they use in growing their own plants. Certainly any soil that you buy off the shelf should be checked for drainage, and, if necessary, amended as recommended for garden soil. If the packaged soil tested has poor drainage, it may not have been sterilized properly, either. The same dense structure that precludes proper drainage can also prevent the penetration of steam or chemicals used in preparing commercial potting soils. In addition, amending packaged potting soils with peat and vermiculite, which contain little or no salts, reduces harmful high salts levels.

To correct these problems and to conserve top soil, researchers have developed excellent potting mixtures that contain no soil. James Boodley and Raymond Sheldrake Jr. of Cornell University pioneered peat-lite mix, an artificial growing media that has won wide acceptance with both professional and amateur growers. Basically composed of fifty per cent sphagnum peat moss and fifty per cent horticultural vermiculite or perlite, peat-lite mixes are readily available, easy to handle, and produce uniform plant growth from year to year. Sterilization is usually unnecessary if reasonable care is taken during mixing and handling.*

Components for Peat-lite Mix

36 litres (1 bushel) shredded sphagnum peat
36 litres (1 bushel) horticultural vermiculite #2, 3, or 4
140 ml (10 tablespoons) finely ground limestone (calcium carbonate)
28 ml (6 teaspoons) of 10-52-10 water-soluble fertilizer with trace elements

Horticultural perlite can be substituted for vermiculite. It is important that the limestone be agricultural grade and finely ground (about the consistency of table salt). Most house plants require a (slightly acid) pH of 5.5 to 6.6. An improper grade of limestone will result in a pH lower than this, making many of the nutrients unavailable to the plant. Dolmitic agricultural limestone also contains twelve per cent magnesium—a beneficial bonus.

---

*Cornell Peat-Lite Mixes for Commercial Plant Growing, Information Bulletin 43, Cornell University, Ithaca, N.Y. (1976).

Add the 10-52-10 water-soluble fertilizer to the nine litres of water used initially to moisten the peat moss. A wheelbarrow properly cleaned with disinfectant is ideal for the mixing operation because it holds the water until absorbed by the peat. Scatter limestone over the measured amounts of moistened peat and vermiculite or perlite and turn with a shovel five times. While mixing should be thorough, unnecessary handling of the moistened mixture will break down the vermiculite to the detriment of porosity and drainage.

Although the mixture is essentially sterile, it can be contaminated. All tools, containers and mixing areas should be washed with a disinfectant. A good disinfectant for floors, tools or mixing equipment can be prepared by using one part bleach in ten parts of water. Small quantities of mixed peat-lite store well in a plastic covered garbage container.

Peat-lite soils also come commercially packaged. Quality control, particle size and soluble salts can vary, however. A brand used for the first time should be given a drainage test. Another test for any potting media is its effect on rooting. A rooted cutting transplanted into a properly moistened potting media at normal room temperature and in adequate light should show new root tips if dug up forty-eight to seventy-two hours later. Ten days after the repotting of a large plant, lift the plant and root ball out of the new pot. Peel away an area of the soil and check for new roots coming out of the old root ball. If new roots are not plainly visible the potting soil is probably too high in salts, and the entire root ball of new and old soil should be leached (see page 29). This uprooting operation to check for root action will not set the plant back if done carefully and it is one of the best tests of a potting media.

The placing of coarse stone or parts of broken clay pots in the bottom of a pot and then putting soil on top of them with the idea of improving drainage is not recommended. This actually hinders the drainage of excess water out of the soil. The movement of water down through a potting soil and out the drainage holes depends on two main factors: the openness or porosity of the soil and the depth. When water is poured onto the surface of the soil in a pot, the porous air spaces form a loosely connected vertical column of water. A greater soil depth provides a longer water column which means greater gravitational pull and faster and more complete drainage. The air spaces in coarse stones or clay shards placed in the bottom of a pot are too large to maintain water column continuity. Therefore they reduce gravitational pull and diminish rather than improve drainage.

Because of the short column of water in the small pots that some plants (such as Baby's Tears) are normally grown in, the soil in the pot may not drain very quickly or completely and a great deal of free water is always left in the pot after it is watered thoroughly. Free water is water which is not adhering directly to the surface of soil particles or water that cannot be absorbed.

To enable you to water thoroughly and yet move out this free water, sit a shallow pot on a 15 or 20 cm pot full of potting soil, sharp concrete or brick sand, pressing it down firmly so that there is contact made from the bottom pot to the soil in the top pot through the drainage holes. If you have two similar-sized pots you can quite easily prove how effective this method is by flooding both pots thoroughly, with one sitting in the sink and the other stacked two pots deep. If you check back twenty to thirty minutes later you will find, by knocking out the root balls, that the one that is sitting on the sand is moist and there is no free water. However, the one that is sitting in the sink will have a readily visible film of free water. If Baby's Tears or other plants in small pots have been giving you trouble, try this method of watering.

If this method has its advantages for plants with fine root systems why not leave the pot sitting on the sand continuously? The problem with this is that the roots will move out of the drainage holes and root into the sand. This access to all the moisture in the sand will promote soft growth which is not desirable for flowering plants in particular. You need the option of withholding water to the point of minor wilting to grow really good-quality flowering plants.

Chapter 2
Watering

Watering Needs

My Scheff plant is so tall now that it brushes the living-room ceiling. In the summer I take it out onto the patio, which has a northern exposure, and it does beautifully, but in the winter it becomes kind of limp. Just recently in addition to the leaves becoming crinkly, droopy and unhappy looking, I have had some on the lower level turn quite yellow and fall off.

The fact that your leaves are drooping indicates that the plant cannot bring up enough water to satisfy its needs. This can be caused by high salts (see pages 30-31), it can be caused by not all the root ball being moistened so that parts of the roots are not functioning properly, or it can be caused by overwatering—the roots are injured when the soil is continually saturated. Your plant is probably in a 35 cm container. Is that correct?

Yes, it is. I put on about a pitcher and a half each time that I water it, about every two weeks.

For that amount of water then, none would come out the drainage hole in the pot.

No.

Then I suspect that the plant is not being thoroughly watered. Parts of the root system are dried out and simply not functioning. I would not increase the frequency of watering, but I would increase the amount. Maybe double. Certainly until the entire soil surface has been flooded and water comes out the drainage hole. Discard this drainage water right after watering.

There are several ways you can test the moisture content of the soil in a pot:

1) If the pot is clay, you can check it by rapping your knuckles on the side of the pot. It will have a hollow ring when it is dry. You can learn to "read" moisture in the soil with this method.

2) Because water evaporates off the surface of the soil, the top dries out sooner than the bottom. Digging down to twenty-five per cent of

the depth of the soil and testing the moisture with your knuckle is a sound method. Bear in mind that most of the root system in a potted plant is in the bottom two thirds of the pot and if this is either too wet or too dry then the plant is going to be adversely affected.

3) If in doubt about any of these methods, and certainly at least once a month, you should tap the root ball out of the pot and check the

With a pot that has tapered sides, removing the plant and root ball is readily accomplished by tapping the pot rim on a counter. This operation is more difficult with a very old plant in a clay pot. The roots cling to the porous clay of the pot and sometimes the plant can only be removed by smashing the pot. Pressing on the flexible bottom of a plastic pot often helps to pop out the root ball.

Before attempting to remove a large plant from its container, prune back any roots that protrude beyond the drainage holes and bind the root ball to the pot. Wiggling the stem while firmly holding the container will loosen the root ball and allow you to lift it out of a tapered container intact.

moisture content of the whole soil ball by feeling it with your hand and by noticing the colour of the soil. It will change from a very light brown through to almost black as the soil goes from dry to wet. You may lose a little bit of the soil off the top of the pot where it isn't completely root bound, but you can prepare for this by putting down newspaper. If a plant is growing properly the root ball should come out and ninety-eight per cent of it will remain intact. The soil should be evenly moist, with no free water dripping out, or visible as a film. Regular checks of the root ball will soon determine whether or not your watering routines are effective.

Regular checking of the root system should be a routine part of the maintenance of all your plants. Healthy plants begin with a sound root system. Knowing what a healthy root system looks like through regular inspection will enable you to spot problems and correct them before they have a damaging effect on the leaves and flowers.

4) Many plant moisture meters do not give a precise reading of the moisture level in your plant's soil. Most moisture meters are really salts meters which depend on the salt content of the soil to conduct an electric current. The strength of this current reads out on a dial or activates a buzzer. Thus wet soil with a very low salt level will read drier than it actually is and may erroneously induce you to water. Conversely, a dry soil with a very high salt content may read wet, deceiving you into withholding water (a condition of very dry soil and high salts further concentrates the salts and is more damaging to the roots).

You can readily check the accuracy of any moisture meter by immersing the probe in distilled water. It should, of course, read "wet" (the meters I have checked read from "barely moist" to "dry"). In my opinion, more judgment is required to use this type of moisture meter than to use the simple look and touch methods mentioned above.

A good check for poor drainage is to pour water onto the surface of the soil of a pot, quickly covering the whole surface with water. That water should disappear in about sixty seconds. Any more than a minute and a half and you have a soil with poor drainage. Repeated applications of water should still disappear off the surface in less than a minute and a half or two minutes, and preferably in about thirty to forty-five seconds.

Overwatering can often cause root rot problems. With root rot, the outer layer of the roots is wrinkled and, in the case of larger roots, loose on the core of the root. In the early stages only sections of the roots may be involved but often the whole root system is dark brown, withered and slimy. Where consistent overwatering is involved the soil ball will smell sour.

If you find root rot present you can use benomyl as a fungicidal drench of the soil. Use the same dilution as recommended for spraying the plants only drench the soil with it as if you were giving the pot a thorough watering. This drenching method may also be used as a preventive measure.

Proper Watering is a Good Growth Regulator

I have a Philodendron that is growing very leggy. It is well watered, has lots of light and is fed periodically. What am I doing wrong?

Is it the type of Philodendron with the ivy-like vine?

Yes. With small, roundish leaves.

Then it is Philodendron scandens oxycardium, sometimes known as Heartleaf Philodendron. What is the distance between the leaves on the stem?

It varies anywhere from 5 to 10 cm. Also the diameter of the stem seems to increase and decrease. It starts out well at the pot level with a fairly thick stock, then goes along a ways and thins out and then comes back into a thick stem.

The plant is responding to the lower light at certain seasons and to the availability of water. You are likely a mathematical waterer, that is, you water every fourth or sixth day or every week regardless of whether or not the soil dries out between waterings.

That may be it. I do tend to do this.

Then you can eliminate the stringy effect by decreasing the watering frequency, particularly during the dull winter months. If you keep the soil constantly moist, you will definitely get stretched, uneven growth with long distances between the leaf nodes in low-light periods. Do not decrease the amount of water that you apply each time (you should always water to a run through), but decrease the frequency to allow drying out of the soil and minor wilting of the plant between waterings. This should not be done to the point where the leaves actually become ragged, but just until they feel limp to the touch. Then water again thoroughly. This will also control the uneven thickness of the stem.

It is the person on the end of the watering hose who can make or break a greenhouse operation. It isn't enough that the plant be kept alive until the time of sale; it must also be attractive. Wise watering can help produce either beautiful plants or unsightly scrocks. (You will not find the word "scrocks" in a dictionary. To the best of my knowledge it was invented by an old friend of mine, Muriel Fretz, who spent many years at a Chrysanthemum grading bench. Anything that wasn't top quality was set aside as a scrock.)

Thorough watering, which involves flooding the whole soil surface until fifteen to twenty per cent runs through the drainage holes, is almost always the correct treatment for plants in a well-drained soil.

But if you find that the distance between the leaf nodes is elongating or the leaf petioles (stems) are too long, then allow minor wilting between waterings. This is particularly effective in the low-light seasons of the year, and will result in thicker, more attractive growth. During the high-light periods of the year the watering frequency can be stepped up. The higher light plus the greater availability of water will produce more abundant growth. Fertilizing can also be done at this time (see Chapter 3).

Leaf-Tip Problems a Symptom of Fluorine

I transplanted a Prayer Plant, and the new leaves seem to be drying at the tips around the edges. What would cause this?

When I hear of leaf-tip problems and leaf edges turning brown on plants like Maranta (Prayer Plant), I am always suspicious of the fluorine that is put in municipal water to prevent tooth decay. Even though they put in only one part per million, prolonged watering over a period of six to eight months with fluoridated water for some reason has a detrimental effect on Maranta, Cordyline, Dracaena, Chlorophytum (Spider Plant), some types of Zebrina (Wandering Jew) and Tradescantia. As the leaves develop, the fluorine collects in the growing tips and eventually proves toxic. The tip of the new leaf turns brown and the leaf dries out. The only way to prevent fluorine damage on the leaves of these plants is to use distilled water, or water from a dehumidifier, air conditioner, rainwater or melted snow.

People Perspire, Horses Sweat, and Plants Guttate

I have a problem with some Impatiens. I brought them in from outside and have been rooting some in earth and some in water. They were doing splendidly but suddenly there are crystal-clear droplets along the stem and around the edges of the leaves. What is this, and what can I do about it?

Those droplets are actually water and will disperse if you touch them. Broadly speaking, the plant is perspiring, although physiologists call it guttating. It is an indication of high humidity around the leaves of the plant and free moisutre at the roots. Of course, with the ones that you are rooting in water, the moisture at the roots is one hundred per cent. If the plants that are in soil are also guttating it means that you are keeping the soil very moist, almost at the saturation point.

Some of the leaves are actually turning brown. Is this caused by this moisture?

Indirectly, yes. When you brought the cuttings in from outdoors there is a distinct possibility that there were fungus-disease spores on the leaves. Under high-humidity conditions these spores can germinate, causing a disease that destroys the leaf tissue (see pages 63-64 on Botrytis). On the Impatiens that you are rooting in soil I would decrease the frequency of misting and watering. Transplant the ones now in water as soon as possible and keep the potting soil a little on the dry side once they are established. Create air movement around your plants by spacing them apart so that the humidity is lowered.

Leaves of many kinds of plants have special structures called hydathodes which permit the extrusion of liquid water under conditions of high water intake and low evaporation. The drops that form at the hydathodes are usually seen in the early morning. Guttation is evidence that the plant has available to it more water than it needs. Wilting, the opposite condition, indicates that the leaves are transpiring more water than the root system can deliver. The cells of the leaf collapse because of the lack of water or low humidity (in the fifteen to twenty per cent range). Higher humidity can be attained with a mechanical humidifier, by covering the plants with clear plastic for brief periods, or by grouping them together.

Humidity and Misting

I received a Boston Fern for Christmas. I have had two before and succeeded in killing both of them. I don't want this to happen again. I would like to know about watering and humidity.

Do you have a humidifier?

Yes. One that is attached to the furnace.

That's fine. You want to have the setting in the forty to fifty per cent bracket. As high as you can tolerate without too much water condensing on the windows on cold nights. Humidity is a critical factor for Ferns. Another way that you can increase the humidity around the plant for at least part of the time is to cover it at night with a plastic cleaner's bag.

What about misting?

Research under control conditions has established that infrequent misting does little or no good because it alters the humidity around the plant for such a short time. In fact, misting can actually harm plants, particularly Ferns. If you mist Ferns with water that contains chlorine the chlorine will gradually build up on the leaves and cause damage. Misting is only truly beneficial in the propogation of plants when you are attempting to put new roots on them.

What is the correct way to water a Fern? The one that I have been given is so large that it fills the pot. It would be impossible to water it without getting water on the crown of the plant. Does this do any harm?

Not at all. In their natural habitat Ferns get drenched entirely. The water should be at room temperature and, at one point or another, cover the whole surface of the soil, particularly around the edges of the pot. Fifteen to twenty per cent should be expelled out the drainage hole and discarded. Bear in mind that a Fern is an epiphyte, or air-root plant. If the soil is kept constantly saturated these very fine air roots will be destroyed. A coarse peat moss is the best medium for Ferns since there are actually large pockets of air along with the soil. The fine brown air roots form in the moist cavities in the soil and draw much of their moisture here. Indeed, much of the trouble that people experience with Ferns is caused by the fact that the plants are grown in a soil that is too compact. Conversely, if the plant is allowed to dry out severely these sensitive roots are destroyed very quickly and the plant will begin to lose leaves. Once a month or so you should tap the plant out of the pot and examine the root system to see if the watering is effective. This has the added benefit of circulating air around the root system and encouraging it to put on new roots.

Ferns (Nephrolepis exaltata) are plants which put on growth by uncoiling the leaf stem. It is essential that you place your Fern so that traffic going by it does not bruise these tender, uncoiling leaf tips. Otherwise growth will be stunted very readily. It is normal, over the period of a year, for some of the older leaves to turn brown and die, but they should always be replaced by new growth. If the older growth is dying more rapidly than new growth is replacing it, look to problems with the root system caused by improper fertilizing or watering, low humidity or low light. If you discover that the root system is weak or injured, help the plant recuperate by up-potting it (plant it in a larger pot without removing the old soil).

Chapter 3
Fertilizing

Overfertilization

I have a problem with a Jade Plant that I bought about six months ago —a fairly mature plant about 60 cm high. It was doing beautifully until about a month ago when it started to drop its leaves. Some of them are shrivelling up and falling off and others are just dropping.

Have you changed its position so that it is receiving less light?

No. If anything it has been receiving more light through this past summer.

Does the container that it is in have drainage holes?

Yes.

And does the water come out through the drainage holes when you water?

Immediately.

Have you done any fertilizing lately?

Yes, I gave it some.

Was it coincidental with the problem?

I think that it may have been.

I strongly suspect that you are overfertilizing it. Probably the plant is growing rather slowly. Plants only need fertilizer when they are putting on new growth. You may be killing it with kindness. A plant growing in a container cannot escape the detrimental effect of excess fertilizer. If excessive fertilizer is added to or released from decomposing organic matter in the soil, it will burn the roots. When the roots are damaged they cannot take up water and the plant reacts by dropping leaves.

Should I remove the soil and repot it?

The answer here is not soil removal and repotting. This will only further damage the injured root system. I would recommend that you try to leach out the extra fertilizer. It will take about two to two and a half hours. Leaching involves putting the pot under a flow of water and over a drain, either in the bathtub, outside, or over a basement drain. The flow rate must be sufficient to keep the entire soil surface covered with tepid water while the water runs through and out the drainage holes without going over the rim of the pot. The plant and soil are left in the container during this process and little or no soil is lost. The water washes away the excess salts, restoring the proper fertility level in the soil so that new growth can begin. The plant should then be exposed to maximum light.

Next to inadequate light, improper fertilizing and watering practices are probably the greatest source of indoor plant problems. Some of the misconceptions about fertilizer stem from the fact that some fertilizers are erroneously called plant foods. Fertilizer is not plant food, but rather contains some of the ingredients from which the plant manufactures its own food. In the presence of adequate light, air, water and fertilizer the plant will manufacture food, or carbohydrates. The carbohydrates provide the energy for plant growth. If we equate fertilizer with plant food, our reaction is to apply fertilizer to a house plant that is not growing. It is far more likely that the lack of growth is related to overfertilization, improper watering or low light. A plant requires little or no fertilizer just to maintain itself in a minimum light situation. It only needs fertilizer to put on new growth.

Outdoors, overfertilization is largely eliminated by rainfall which washes the fertilizer down into the subsoil. Indoors, particularly in the winter, the light levels are such that the plant is barely able to maintain itself, let alone put on new growth. Under these conditions little or no fertilizer is required. Most house plants come into the home in a soil that contains enough fertilizer to carry that plant for several weeks or even months. But if you buy a plant in the summer when the light levels are high and the plant continues to grow actively, then yes, it will require some fertilizer.

How can you tell if a plant is overfertilized? There are several symptoms. First the green portion of the foliage will become very dark. Then growth will cease and the foliage will remain limp when there is moisture obviously present in the soil. Up to this point little or no harm may have been done. These symptoms can appear with an application of unneeded fertilizer or a drop in light. They are, however, a warning that no fertilizer should be applied. If fertilizer is applied, the salts level will rise to the point where the roots are seriously burned. The plant can no longer take up water through the injured root system, the leaves begin to turn yellow or brown, and with a succulent plant like Jade, they wrinkle. Eventually they dry and fall off.

Don't assume, however, because you do little or no fertilizing that the fertility level is correct. Water continuously evaporating from the surface of the soil can leave behind a salt that is injurious when washed down to the roots. Soil, in decomposing, also releases plant nutrients in a salt form and unless the plant is growing rapidly enough to use these they too can build up.

To prevent overfertilization you must not only constantly monitor the appearance of the plant leaves but also the root system (see page 20). One of the first signs of high salts is the disappearance of the smaller root hairs which extract most of the water and fertilizer from the soil. Don't be misled by the fact that there are large roots readily visible. These larger roots mainly act as carrier roots which conduct water up into the plant. It is the small and, in some plants, almost fuzz-like hair roots that are really picking up moisture and nutrients and are the first injured by high salts. In healthy plants there should be a growing root tip which in most cases is white (in Ferns it is either a chartreuse colour or brown).

In high-salts situations the larger roots will look wrinkled and if the salts are very high they may look completely dry and withered even though the soil around them is moist (the salt level around the root is so high that it is actually pulling moisture out of the roots).

On larger plants you may be able to disengage one of the larger roots, possibly two to three millimeters in diameter, from the soil ball. Try to slip the skin on that root. If the skin adheres firmly to the inner part of the root stem, then you have a healthy root. But if that outer skin slips on the inner core, then the root has been damaged.

The Dangers of Long-Lasting Fertilizers

I have a Weeping Fig, and boy, is it weeping.

You mean the leaves are weeping off?

Yes. It's in such sad shape. I have had it a couple of weeks and it is losing all its leaves. They are turning brown and dropping off. I'm desperate. What on earth is the matter with it?

What light is it receiving?

I have it in my sitting room and it is right in the front window where it gets lots of morning light.

What type of container is it in?

It's a black plastic container with holes in the bottom.

Then this is probably the original container and soil that the plant was grown in in Florida. When you water it can you see the water go out the drainage holes?

I haven't looked, to tell you the truth.

How large is the plant?

Oh, it was a beautiful big hearty plant about three metres high when I brought it home.

The problem could be not enough water. If you are not applying sufficient water to run ten to twenty per cent out of the drainage holes then you may not be putting on enough to wet the soil ball, and some of the roots cannot pick up water. The above-ground reaction of the plant to an excessively dry condition is to shed leaves. The other problem could be too high a salts level. Are there any tiny plastic pellets on the surface of the soil?

Yes.

These tiny pellets are used in Florida to fertilize tropical plants such as Ficus benjamina over a long period of time. These fertilizer pellets are designed to release a prescribed amount of fertilizer per day so that heavy rain cannot leach it out. But they can become really harmful when the plant in the home isn't growing rapidly enough to absorb this fertilizer and there is no rain to leach out any excess. I would suggest that you take this plant and leach it(see page 29). Should you continue to lose leaves after leaching, the plant can be assisted in refoliating by misting it, wrapping it in clear plastic such as a cleaner's bag, and leaving it in bright diffused light in a warm location (as high as 25°C). This process increases the humidity around the branches and buds of the plant and it will usually refoliate in a short time, once the salts level in the soil is correct. I would not do this, however, unless you lose ninety to one hundred per cent of the leaves. Otherwise I would just allow the plant to sit in normal light and it should refoliate within a month or two.

The presence of long-lasting fertilizer pellets indicates improper acclimatizing by the grower and retailer. Improperly acclimatized foliage plants are the bane of the plant industry. For long-lasting satisfaction green plants must be purchased from reliable suppliers. With the sudden upsurge in popularity of house plants many merchandisers have jumped into the business of selling them. The poor quality of the merchandise leads to widespread problems when the plants are taken into the home.

Tropical plants such as the Ficus benjamina, grown in full sunlight of Florida, have a type of cell structure that actually precludes light entering the leaves, except in very small quantities. When you realize that full sunlight in Florida could be as much as 12,000 or 15,000 foot candles and that in the winter the light in the windows of our homes reaches only 200 to 300 foot candles, then you begin to understand the wide spread that the plant has to tolerate. The inherent structure of the leaves that keeps out most of the brilliant sunlight of Florida will also cut out even the little light that it receives in the home. The functions of the leaves cease because the light cannot penetrate the leaf to generate food production.

Many of the discount stores and fly-by-night operators in the plant business buy cheaper, full-sun produced plants in Florida, truck them up and offer them to the public without any acclimatizing whatsoever. Then you get the unhappy phenomenon of defoliation.

Good plant dealers buy their large plants from operators who have grown them under a saran netting that cuts out up to eighty per cent of the Florida light. The leaves of these shade-grown plants have a cell structure that allows greater light penetration, enabling these plants to make the transition from the 3,000 foot candles of the shade structure to the 300 foot candles of our homes.

Reliable growers will lower the light of shade-grown plants even further in a northern greenhouse, so that they can be moved into your home with little leaf loss. They will also remove any long-lasting fertilizer pellets from the soil and thoroughly leach the soil for at least two to three hours to reduce salts levels.

This procedure of preparing plants for the home is called acclimatizing. It involves establishing the correct salts content in the soil, lowering the light levels, inducing defoliation of any leaves that cannot make the transition into the home, and cleaning up the plant as far as insects and fungus are concerned. It takes six to eight weeks. Plants that come directly from Florida, off a truck, into a discount house, and are sold, do not go through this process and subsequently the home owner can have great difficulty with them.

Choosing a Fertilizer

What is the best fertilizer to use on my house plants when they are on my shaded patio in the summer?

Are the plants and soil exposed to rain?

Yes, the shadow is cast by a large tree nearby, not a roof.

I would let the first rains of June do a good leaching job and wait for new growth to appear before applying any fertilizer. Because the plants are exposed to rain, the most convenient form would be a pelletized controlled-release fertilizer with approximately a 14-14-14 formulation. Apply it to the surface of the soil at the prescribed rate based on the size of the container. This type of fertilizer will give a steady release of nutrients all summer. Scrape the pellets off in mid-August and discard them so that the plants are not brought back into the lower light of your home with too high a level of fertilizer.

Fertilizer has two basic sources: organic and inorganic. Some organic sources of plant nutrients are compost, animal manure, fish emulsions, reclaimed sewage sludge, animal bone meal and blood, and seaweed. Chemical plant nutrients come from many sources but regardless of the source, all nutrients must ultimately be in a water-soluble form to be taken up by the root system.

Organic sources of plant nutrients are very unpredictable when placed in a potting soil. For example, you may realize that a plant requires phosphorus because of deficiency symptoms evident in the plant or a complete soil analysis, but if you applied bone meal to the soil of a container-grown plant, it might well be six months to a year before soil bacteria and micro-organisms change the phosphorus in the bone meal to a form which can be used by the plant. With a plant growing in a container with a restricted soil volume and root system it is essential that nutrients be applied in the correct amount and at the time when the plant needs them, otherwise over-or underfertilizing can result. For this reason, organic sources of plant nutrients are not generally as reliable as chemical fertilizers for use on house plants.

Should a drainage water sample or an examination of the root system and a rapid growth rate indicate the need for fertilizer, a number of types are available.

1) I would recommend **controlled-release fertilizer** for plants that are going to be exposed to rain during the summer simply because this fertilizer only releases a predictable amount of the nutrients over a specified period of time. The fertilizer cannot be leached out of the soil by a sudden thunderstorm. One type of controlled-release fer-

tilizer (Agriform) is available in a large capsule form which is inserted just below the surface of the soil and can be selected for a six-month or two-year release period. Osmocote and Precise are water-soluble fertilizers pelletized with a plastic membrane. The fertilizer is dissolved when moisture initially penetrates the membrane of the pellets and is then released through this plastic membrane at a controlled rate by an osmotic process.

The advantage of controlled-release fertilizer capsules or pellets is that only one application is needed for the whole season. All the grower has to do is water the plant when required. However, the same fertilizer in an indoor situation can be a menace. As long as there is moisture present in the soil, the fertilizer is released according to schedule. Unless the plant is growing actively and needs that fertilizer, very soon it is receiving too much, and the root system is injured.

Should you wish to experiment with one of these controlled-release fertilizers indoors, do not incorporate it into the soil when planting. Always place it on the surface. Then you can scrape it off and leach out any of the excess fertilizer if necessary.

2) Granular fertilizer (generally the type used outdoors on gardens and lawns) varies in solubility depending on the elements involved. It is because of this variability that we seldom use granular fertilizer on indoor plants or incorporate it in potting soils. It is far safer and more precise to use a water-soluble fertilizer as the plant requires it. The only exception to this is granular superphosphate (20% phosphorus). It has a slow, steady release rate and, in the correct amount, can be safely incorporated into potting soil at time of mixing.

3) A good **water-soluble fertilizer** should be *fully* soluble. Many brands on the market (not necessarily the cheaper ones) do not completely dissolve, and you have no way of knowing what portion of the fertilizer has been left undissolved. Because the elements in a good soluble fertilizer are completely water soluble, mixing and application can be done with precision and the chances of over-fertilizing are minimal.

Fertilizer Contents

While it is the portion of the plant above the soil line that you enjoy, only a healthy root system can extract the elements your plants require for growth. Carbon, hydrogen and oxygen are readily obtained with proper watering and a normal atmospheric environment.

Three of the six major chemical elements that the plant requires—nitrogen, phosphorus, potassium—have to be applied as a fertilizer. The percentage of the water-soluble portion of each of these elements is what you will find printed on any fertilizer container, and always in that order (e.g. 20-20-20).

Calcium, magnesium and sulphur are also required for plant growth. Calcium and magnesium should be added to potting soils at the time of mixing in the form of finely ground dolmitic limestone. Sulphur is usually found in sufficient quantities in the garden soil portion of a potting soil, often brought down out of the atmosphere in industrial areas by rainfall. In synthetic potting media containing no soil, it can be obtained by incorporating superphosphate granular fertilizer at the time of mixing.

There are, however, trace or minor elements that are also essential for balanced plant growth. If your potting soil contains loam top soil (good garden soil) then generally these elements are already present. However, many potting soils are almost completely synthetic with little or no top soil. Very successful results can be obtained with the synthetic mixtures provided trace elements are available in the fertilizer you use. The trace elements are manganese, iron, boron, zinc, copper, molybdenum and chlorine. These minor elements are generally not available in either long-lasting controlled-release fertilizers or granular fertilizers. However, they should be present in any good water-soluble fertilizer and the amount should be expressed as a percentage of the whole and printed clearly on the container. The inclusion of soluble trace elements in a water-soluble fertilizer greatly adds to its value.

There is no magic in fertilizers. Their value depends on the amount they contain of the elements outlined above and the form that they are in. The cheapest is the granular form and this is quite adequate for most outdoor applications. The controlled-release and water-soluble fertilizers are convenient, but more expensive. If you are doing comparative shopping for a water-soluble fertilizer you can determine the best value by taking the three numbers that indicate the analysis of the fertilizer, adding them up and dividing them into the cost per kilogram. This will give you the price of a unit of fertilizer.

Most water-soluble fertilizers come in a crystal form and should readily and completely dissolve in tepid water at prescribed rates. Any residue that settles out of the solution after it has stood for a day is the sign of an inferior product. Water-soluble fertilizers sold in liquid form are always more expensive than crystal fertilizers with the only advantage of taking a little less stirring to mix with water.

A ratio of equal parts (e.g. 20-20-20) of the major elements of a water-soluble fertilizer is adequate for most house plants. It is helpful to realize that nitrogen generally contributes to the green growth of the plant, i.e. the size and number of leaves and stems. Phosphorus contributes to the root development of the plant and its ability to reach out and pick up plant nutrients. Potassium or potash contributes to the stiffness of the stem, the colour, quality and texture of the blooms, and fragrance.

The most accurate way to determine the nutrients in the soil is to take a sample to a soil testing laboratory. (Soil test labs are often operated by provincial or state departments of agriculture at a nominal cost.) This usually involves testing for the major elements plus pH and total soluble salts. The lab report normally includes a table of acceptable nutrient levels that can be compared with the levels in your soil.

A less definitive but still effective way to determine fertility levels is to take a drainage-water sample. This is done by watering to a run through with the tap water you usually use for your plants. Collect eight to ten millilitres of the first water that comes out the drainage hole. Take this, along with an equal amount of the source water, to a plant store or garden centre that has a solubridge for measuring the electrical conductivity of a salt solution. This instrument gives a read-out of the total dissolved salts, which is compared with a test of the source water. Some garden centres will do this for free as a service to their customers.

However, even with the evidence of these tests, the condition of the root system should still be determined (see page 20).

Plant Nutrient Deficiency Symptoms

The leaves and general growth of the plant also manifest nutrient deficiency symptoms which are recognizable with experience.

Nitrogen — The growth rate of plants with nitrogen deficiency is greatly restricted. The entire plant may be light green or yellow in colour with reduced leaf size if the plant has been grown continuously under low nitrogen conditions. If the plant is suffering from nitrogen deficiency after a period of normal growth, the lower leaves will be light green or yellow while the upper leaves appear nearly normal.

Phosphorus — One of the most common symptoms of phosphorus deficiency is the abnormal development of anthocyanin pigment which causes a purple coloration particularly on the undersides of leaves. A much-reduced growth rate is also evident. Foliage may remain dark green with lower leaves sometimes yellow between the veins.

Potassium — The lower leaves are the first to be affected and show a large number of small mottled areas, primarily near the edges, which soon die.

Calcium — The shoot tip becomes yellow, twisted and finally dark brown and dies. The young leaves nearest the shoot may also be affected Root growth is severely restricted and abnormal.

Magnesium — The area between the leaf veins turns light green, yellow, and finally white. Leaf margins may curl up or down or leaves may pucker. Leaves die in later stages.

Iron — The tip of the shoot stays alive and new upper leaves turn yellow between the veins (large veins remain green). Edges and tips of leaves may die.

Sulphur — The tip of the shoot stays alive and upper leaves turn light green. Leaf veins are lighter than surrounding areas.

Manganese — The tip of the shoot stays alive and new upper leaves have dead spots over the surface. The leaf may appear netted because of small veins remaining green.

Boron — The tip of the shoot dies and stems and petioles are brittle.

Zinc and copper are normally in tap water in sufficient quantities as impurities and chlorine is amply supplied as an additive in some municipal water.

Caution: The symptoms of overfertilization are often similar to the plant nutrient deficiencies listed above. However, with underfeeding, the root system shows none of the damaged symptoms outlined earlier. Severe over-or underwatering will also injure the root system, resulting in leaf problems that can be mistaken for nutrient deficiency symptoms. Do a drainage water test or a complete soil analysis if the plant is valuable.

How Often to Apply Fertilizer

There is no fixed rule to determine how often fertilizer should be applied. If your examination of the root system indicates healthy activity and you observe any of the deficiency symptoms apply a water-soluble fertilizer, allowing two to three weeks for a response. Repeat every two to three weeks until normal growth is resumed. If there is no visible reaction then fertilize at every watering until there is evident response. Then begin to stretch the intervals between fertilizing.

How Much Fertilizer to Apply

All brands of fertilizer packaged for domestic use have standard dilution recommendations: follow these recommendations and if in doubt use half the amount suggested. Use the fertilizer solution in place of a normal watering. Never fertilize a wilted plant. Wilting is a sign of high salts at the root system, loss of roots due to suffocation from flooding, or excessively dry soil. Fertilizing can do nothing but aggravate the first two situations and in the latter case should be preceded by watering and time to allow the plant to pick up the water.

The limiting factor with growing most plants in the home is not usually lack of fertilizer but light, particularly in the winter months. If your light source is sunlight, fertilize in high-light, high-growth periods and discontinue as light decreases. Leach thoroughly for two to three hours at least once during the dark months. If the light source is entirely artificial, then growth and therefore fertilizer requirements should be uniform throughout the year. However, bear in mind that soils with organic content usually release plant nutrients as the organic matter decomposes. The rate of this release may provide sufficient nutrients for some months after repotting.

Chapter 4
Lighting

Artificial Lighting

I am concerned about foliage plants in an office where the lights are on twenty-four hours a day. Should they really be kept where the lights are on all the time?

Most foliage plants will do very well with twenty-four hours of fluorescent light a day. The only exception that I know of is Cissus rhombifolia (Grape Ivy). Left in light over eighteen hours a day the plant seems to turn brown and deteriorate rapidly.

A hen will lay more eggs if kept in light twenty-four hours a day and foliage plants, aside from the exception noted above, will put on more growth if exposed to constant light. Most offices are lit with cool white fluorescent lights, which produce the best growth on tropical foliage plants. They will do just as well under cool white fluorescent as under grow lights or colour-corrected fluorescent grow lights.

If the light intensity is not sufficient for the plant to put on new growth, you can improve the light conditions by increasing the duration of light. If the lights can only operate ten or twelve hours a day, then you can increase the intensity of light that the plants receive, that is, increase the wattage or number of bulbs or put the plants closer to the light source. As you increase the intensity or the duration or both, the carbohydrate production in the plant increases, promoting growth.

Incandescent lights can also be used to increase light intensity, but bear in mind that there is a lot of the red portion of the light spectrum in incandescent light. This is heat, so you should check carefully that the plant is not receiving too much heat from the bulbs. Incandescent plant grow lights with reduced red-ray emission allow you to install the bulb closer to the plant without over-heating the leaves.

Plants such as Dracaena marginata with their graceful, slender stems and narrow leaves are not only decorative but are also quite practical because the upper leaves do not prevent light from reaching the leaves lower down. This, plus the plant's inherent adaptability to low light, explains why they are so popular in many offices.

If some of your plants are doing well in a given location, and those in a different spot are not doing so well, you could rotate into the good location and bring the others into the more difficult environment.

Should they begin to deteriorate, move them back to the better location. In this way you would give all your plants a couple of weeks where the conditions are more difficult.

Cut-Leaf Philodendron

Some of the leaves on my Cut-leaf Philodendron are almost solid while others have deep serrations. Some leaves are somewhere in between. What is the cause of this?

The Cut-leaf Philodendron will grow in low light, but if the light is borderline then the plant does not develop the characteristic deep serrations on the leaves. You will find that it will produce plain leaves during periods of very low winter light and that the serrations will begin to appear again in new leaves as the light intensity increases in the spring and summer. Try placing the plant where it receives more light in the winter time and then bring it back from the light source in the summer.

OPPOSITE. *The leaves of the Cut-leaf Philodendron have deep serrations when the plant is growing under optimum light. Plain-edged leaves are produced under low light.*

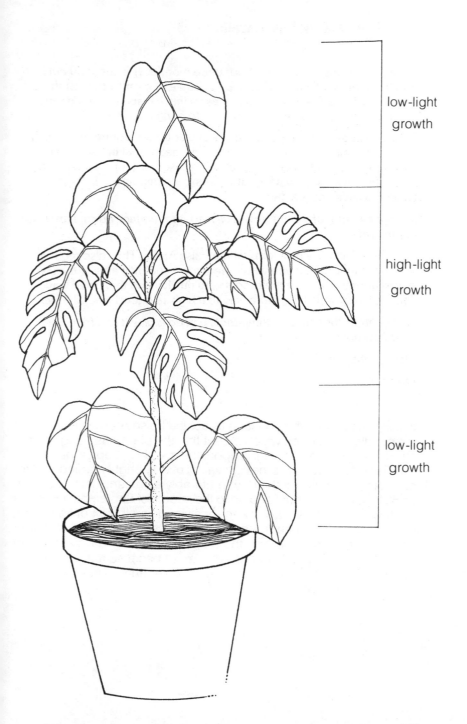

low-light
growth

high-light
growth

low-light
growth

43

High Light Plants: False Aralia

I have had a False Aralia for about three months. It is about 50 cm high and it was in excellent condition for a couple of months but just the last few weeks it has been losing its leaves so that it is spindly and dreary looking. Is there anything that I can do to bring it back?

False Aralia is one of those sub-tropical plants that requires bright light just to maintain itself, let alone grow. This means that in the winter months you should place it directly in an east, south or west window or in an office in a location where it is getting a minimum of 150 foot candles twelve hours a day.

It is right in front of a window but all my windows face north. I am in an apartment.

Yes, this could pose problems with a False Aralia. They also require very even moisture. If you water them too frequently and/or the soil drains poorly, they lose their roots very quickly and then shed leaves. They will respond in the same way to a high salts level (see Chapter 3).

So you think that the best thing that I can do is give it to a friend with a south window.

That's right.

Oh dear.

It is significant that the question about the False Aralia was asked in the middle of October, which meant that the plant was bought in the middle of July. Trouble began about the middle of September.

A False Aralia requires the equivalent of very bright reading light for at least twelve hours of the day, preferably eighteen, just to maintain itself. In July and August and up to the middle of September even in a north window it must have been receiving this amount of light, for it survived well. But once the middle of September passed, the light intensity began to drop and the number of cloudy days increased dramatically. The plant started to fall apart because the light energy was reduced below the compensation point (the point at which the plant was able to maintain itself).

Symptoms of Low Light

I have a Lipstick Plant. I don't know if you have heard of it before.

Yes, I have. The botanical name is Aeschynanthus pulcher.
In the summer it grows fine outdoors but when I bring it in in the winter it only develops tiny leaves and I don't know why.

When you put it outdoors, is it in sun or shade?
It is in the shade.

That is the correct place. It wants subdued summer light. The limiting factor could be the amount of light that it receives in the winter. When it is outdoors is it exposed to rain?
Not actually but when it does rain I take it out and put it in the rain.

There are probably two factors at work here. When you put the plant outdoors in the summer and expose it to rain it leaches the nutrients out of the soil. Then when you bring it back indoors it has the additional problem of low light. During the summer months when you allow the plant to be exposed to rain, fertilize it with a water-soluble fertilizer at least once a month, or after every heavy rain. When you bring it indoors you should not have to fertilize again for the rest of the winter. Make sure, however, that you put it in a location indoors where it receives a maximum amount of light. Near a window facing east, west or south.

A friend from Inuvik once described the effect of the long nights on herself and her neighbours in that Arctic community. There was a general sense of depression and listlessness. She found herself walking a quarter of a mile out of her way through the cold Arctic night to avoid having to speak to a close friend. A similar depressive effect occurs with plants under the low-light conditions that exist in the winter in our temperate climates.

Plants have only a limited ability to store plant food. Once this is exhausted then light is required to manufacture more. Without adequate light, the "factory" that exists in the leaves of every plant grinds to a halt.

Having checked for active roots, correct and consistent soil moisture, and absence of insects, then any foliage problems are likely caused by low light during winter months. (It is important to realize how drastically the light level is lowered when a plant is brought indoors. On a bright summer day in the full shade of a large tree a light meter will probably show a reading of 3,000 foot candles. Yet in the east, west or south window of a home a light meter reading taken right next to the window on a dull winter day would be as low as 100 foot candles.)

Symptoms of Low Light

1) A gradual or drastic slowing of growth rate until there is a complete absence of new growth.

2) New leaves formed under low-light conditions will be a paler colour and thinner in structure. Plants with coloured leaves (such as Croton) lose their brilliance and revert to green, or the leaves simply fall off. Older leaves further from the light source or shaded by other leaves turn yellow and fall off. The death rate of these older leaves accelerates and begins to overtake the production of newer leaves, leaving a net loss in leaf area.

3) Leaf petioles (stems) will be longer and weaker, and the length of the stem between leaves elongates. A graphic example of this is Baby's Tears which, under sufficient light, will have each set of leaves very close to the next set on the stem. Under low light it will develop a very long, stringy vine between sets of leaves. If, however, the light becomes excessive the leaves actually burn. This trait makes Baby's Tears a natural light meter.

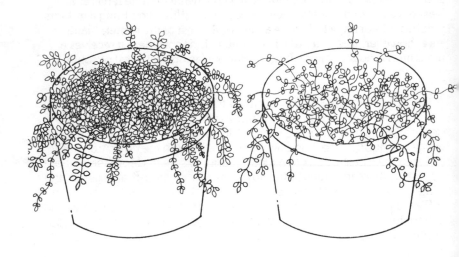

Correct light produces dense growth on Baby's Tears. Long, stringy stems with long spaces between the tiny leaves indicate low light if watering practices are correct. Exposure to overly intense light will stunt growth and, if too strong, will burn the leaves.

4) Stems of upright plants become weak and need support.

5) Flowering plants are unable or reluctant to set buds. Buds are very slow to develop, sometimes turn yellow, abort and fall off. Flower stems are weak with smaller, paler blooms lacking substance and durability.

6) Plant parts propagated from a plant grown in low light tend to have a higher mortality rate. Rooting is very slow and erratic.

7) Plants are more susceptible to fungus diseases such as mildew, and to other forms of disease.

8) Hairy Cacti such as Old Man of the Andes (Oreocereus celsianus) go or grow bald.

9) Flowers of plants such as the pot mum, when purchased half out, fail to open properly and the centres of the blooms partially opened turn black and rot.

10) Plants with a normally branching growth habit do not branch out.

Selecting the Right Plant for the Light Situation

I have a bay window which faces south and I would like to fill it with plants. There is a three-story house about eight metres away and there is a big tree in the yard so I do not get direct summer sun. Is it a good spot for African Violets?

It sounds ideal for African Violets. The only time of the year that the light might become too intense for them is just before that tree leafs out in late March or April. The petiole or stem of the leaf of the African Violet is a good light monitor. Very short leaf petioles packed tightly around the pot indicate that you are approaching maximum light. Long, thin leaf petioles indicate too low a light level.

Are there any other flowering plants that would do well in my bay window?

Episcia form satellite plants on umbilical cords similar to Spider Plants and flower on the parent plant as well as on the new little plantlets. The flowers are single, about 2 cm in diameter, ranging in colour from white and yellow through to red. The green leaves have a copper and sometimes even a pink and purple undertone. Columneas would also do very well in this situation, and they have tiny little tubular flowers in varying shades of pink, red and white. On some varieties the foliage is hairy, similar to the Episcia and African Violet. Others are quite glossy and elliptical in shape and trail down like Ivy. Both these species should do well in a window such as yours. Almost any of the green trailing plants would also do quite well: Ivy, Spider Plant, Pothos, Philodendron cordatum. In short, your window can become a source of beauty and inspiration.

Yes. It is an older house and the window sill is about one metre off the ground. It has built-in cupboards with ceramic tile tops so it is a beautiful spot.

It sounds delightful. Practically any foliage plant would do well here. The only time that you would have to be careful is in the early spring just before the leaves come on that tree when you may have to put on sheers to cut the light intensity a bit. Use your African Violets as check plants. If the foliage starts to lose colour and the growth becomes very compact and rossetty, it is a sign that you are getting too much light.

Light Requirements of House Plants

Lack of light is often the limiting factor in the survival of house plants, particularly during the low-light winter months experienced in much of North America. Research has recently begun to determine the minimum and optimum requirements of a broad range of house plants. The following list is based on recent research. Where this is not yet available it is compiled empirically and may change as our experience increases.

Plants are listed in order of those tolerating the lowest light to those requiring higher light. At the low reading in each group the plant may only survive with no new growth during the winter months, but will thrive during the high-light period of the year. If the energy source is artificial light and it is consistently at or near the lowest level given, then plants will only be able to maintain themselves. Poor maintenance, drafts and low humidity will also shorten the life of the plant.

If you are considering purchasing a large plant for a specific place in your home or office, the most reliable method is to take readings with a General Electric Model 214 light meter, directing the meter toward the light source from the position where the plant will be placed. A good plant outlet should have these meters available to customers on a deposit and return basis. Take several readings, particularly on dull winter days, and average the results. Under artificial light, the following approximate equivalents are given:

Sewing, accounting, fine work . . . . 200 foot candles
Department stores . . . . 100-150 foot candles
Comfortable reading light, bathroom . . . . . 75-100 foot candles
Malls, hallways, stairways . . . . 25-50 foot candles

Group A   25 to 250 foot candles

Plants tolerant of lowest light situations in dull corners or more than three metres from the window. On a dull winter day with drapes and sheers open, this light level would require you to turn on lights to read comfortably. Plants may have to be turned every couple of weeks if the light is available only from one direction, so that all the leaves receive light at some time.

AGLAONEMA
(ahg-la-oh-NEEM-a) most species   e.g. Chinese Evergreen

CISSUS rhombifolia
(SISS-us rom-bi-FOL-ee-a)   Grape Ivy

PHILODENDRON scandens oxycardium
(fill-o-DEN-dron SKAN-dens ox-i-
KAR-dee-um)   •   Heartleaf Philodendron

DRACAENA godseffiana
(dra-SEE-na god-seff-ee-AH-na)   Dracaena Florida Beauty

EPIPREMNUM aureum
(ep-i-PREMM-num ow-RAY-um)   Pothos

SANSEVIERIA
(san-se-VEER-ee-a) most species   e.g. Snake Plant

PEPEROMIA
(pep-er-OM-ee-a) most species   e.g. Emerald Ripple

CHAMAEDOREA elegans 'bella'
(kam-ee-DOR-eh-a EL-e-gans BELL-a)   Neanthe Bella Palm

CHAMAEDOREA erumpens
(kam-ee-DOR-eh-a eh-RUMP-enz)   Bamboo Palm

CHAMAEDOREA seifrizii
(kam-ee-DOR-eh-a sigh-FRITZ-eye)   Reed Palm

DRACAENA deremensis
(dra-SEE-na day-re-MEN-sis)   e.g. Janet Craig

DRACAENA fragrans massangeana
(dra-SEE-na FRAY-grans mas-
san-gee-AH-nah)   Corn Plant

HOWEIA forsteriana
(HOW-ee-a for-ster-i-AH-na)   Kentia Palm

SPATHIPHYLLUM clevelandii
(spath-i-FIL-um KLEEV-land-eye)   Peace Lily

CYCAS revoluta
(SIGH-kuss rev-oh-LUTE-ah)   Sago Palm

ASPIDISTRA elatior
(ass-pi-DISS-trah ee-LAYT-ee-or)   Cast Iron Plant

CRASSULA argentea
(krass-OOL-a ar-GENT-ee-a)   Jade Plant

LIVISTONA chinensis
(liv-i-STOH-na kin-EN-sis)   Chinese Fan Palm

Group B   75-250 foot candles

Plants tolerant of diffused light in an east or west window with sheers pulled, but open in the months of November, December, January and February, or placed within three metres of a sheerless window, but not in direct sunshine, except in November, December and January. Or in artificial light of a store or office where the lights operate for at least twelve hours a day, and preferably eighteen. Again, the plant may have to be turned every couple of weeks if light is available only from one direction so that all leaves receive light at some time.

POLYSTICHUM tsus-simense (po-LISS-ti-kum tsus si-MENS)	Korean Rock Fern	
NEPHROLEPIS exaltata (neff-ro-LEP-is egs-al-TAHT-a)	Boston Fern	H
SELAGINELLA (sell-ah-ji-NELL-a) most species	e.g. Moss Fern	T
PLATYCERIUM (plaa-tee-SEER-ee-um)	Staghorn Fern	H
PELLAEA rotundifolia (pel-EE-ah ro-tund-i-FOH-lee-a)	Cliffbrake Fern	H
ADIANTUM hispidulum (ah-dee-AHN-tum hiss-PID-u-lum)	Australian Maidenhair	H
ADIANTUM decorum (ah-dee-AHN-tum deh-KOR-um)	Maidenhair Fern	T
ASPLENIUM nidus (as-PLEN-ee-um NID-us)	Bird's Nest Fern	H
PTERIS cretica (TEER-is KRET-i-kah)	Table Fern	H
HEMIGRAPHIS colorata (hee-mi-GRAF-is ko-lor-AH-ta)	Waffle Plant	
PHILODENDRON (fill-o-DEN-dron) many species	e.g. 'Emerald Queen'	
PHOENIX roebelenii (FEE-nicks ro-bel-EN-eye)	Date Palm	

T=Must have high humidity of terrarium situation to survive.
H=Must have humidity of at least forty per cent.

CHRYSALIDOCARPUS lutescens (kris-al-id-o-KAR-pus loo-TESS-ens)	Areca Palm	
FATSHEDERA lizei (fahts-HED-er-a LITZ-eye)	Pagoda Tree	
SOLEIROLIA soleirolii (so-LAYR-ol-ee-a so-LAYR-ol-eye)	Baby's Tears	
STENANDRIUM lindenii (sten-AND-ree-um LINN-den-eye)		T
PELLIONIA daveauana (pell-ee-OH-nee-a daa-voh-AH-nah)	Watermelon Begonia	
DIEFFENBACHIA amoena (dee-fen-BAK-ee-a a-MEEN-a)	Dumb Cane	
HEDERA helix (HED-er-a HEE-licks) most varieties	Ivy	
FITTONIA verschaffeltii argyroneura (fi-TON-ee-a ver-SHAFF-elt-eye ar- gi-ro-NOOR-a)	Nerve Plant	
MARANTA (mar-AHNT-a)	e.g. Prayer Plant	
CALATHEA insignis (kal-aa-THEE-a in-sig-nis)	e.g. Peacock Plant	
ANTHURIUM scherzerianum (an-THOO-ree-um share-zare- ee-AH-num)	Anthurium	H
SYNGONIUM podophyllum (sin-GOHN-ee-um po-do-FIL-um)	Nephthytis	
ZAMIA furfuracea (ZAME-ee-a fur-fur-ACE-ee-a)	Jamaica Sago Tree	
BRASSAIA actinophylla (bruss-EYE-a ak-tin-o-FIL-a)	Schefflera	
FICUS retusa nitida (FYK-us re-TOOS-a NIT-i-da)	Indian Laurel	
BEGONIA rex (beg-OHN-ya reks)	most varieties	
BEGONIA foliosa (beg-OHN-ya fol-ee-OH-sa)	Trailing Fernleaf	
CRYPTANTHUS bivittatus (krip-TAHN-thus biv-i-TAT-us)	Earth Star	

PILEA microphylla (pi-LAY-a mi-kro-FIL-a)	Artillery Plant
PILEA cadierei (pi-LAY-a ka-dee-AIR-ee-eye)	Aluminum Plant
PILEA involucrata (pi-LAY-a in-vol-oo-KRAH-ta)	Friendship Plant
PILEA depressa (pi-LAY-a deh-PRESS-a)	Creeping Pilea or Miniature Peperomia
CRASSULA cultrata (KRASS-ool-a kul-TRAH-ta)	Propeller Plant
CRASSULA lycopodioides (KRASS-ool-a lye-koh-poh-dee-o-EED-es)	Watchchain Jade Plant
CRASSULA portulacea (KRASS-ool-a por-too-LA-kee-a)	Crosby's Compacta
CRASSULA tetragona (KRASS-ool-a te-tra-GON-a)	Pinetree Jade
PLECTRANTHUS australis (plek-TRAN-thus ows-TRAL-is)	Swedish Ivy
DRACAENA reflexa (dra-SEE-na reh-FLEX-a)	Malaysian Dracaena
DRACAENA thalioides (dra-SEE-na thal-ee-o-EED-es)	Lance Dracaena
MIKANIA ternata (mi-KAHN-ee-a ter-NAHT-a)	Plush Vine
FICUS elastica (FYK-us eh-LAHS-ti-ka)	Rubber Plant
FICUS lyrata (FYK-us li-RAHT-a)	Fiddle Leaf Fig
FICUS benjamina (FYK-us ben-ja-MEE-na)	Weeping Fig
FICUS pumila (FYK-us poo-MIL-a)	Creeping Fig
HAWORTHIA limifolia keithii (ha-WORTH-ee-a lim-i-FOL-ee-a KEITH-eye)	Haworthia

CYRTOMIUM falcatum
(sir-TOM-ee-um fal-KAT-um)   Holly Fern   H

TOLMIEA menziesii
(TOLL-me-a men-ZEES-eye)   Piggyback Plant

COLUMNEA
(ko-LUM-nee-a) most varieties   e.g. Chocolate Soldier

ABUTILON
(ah-BEU-till-on)   Flowering Maple

AZALEA
(ah-ZAY-lee-a)   Azalea

TRADESCANTIA fluminensis
(trahd-es-KAHN-tee-a floom-i-NEN-sis) Wandering Jew

ANANAS comosus
(a-NAHN-as ko-MOS-us)   Pineapple Plant

APHELANDRA squarrosa
(ahf-el-AHN-dra squa-ROH-sa)   Zebra Plant

PANDANUS veitchii
(pan-DANN-us VEE-cheye)   Screw Pine

CORDYLINE terminalis
(kor-di-LIN-eh ter-min-AHL-is)   Hawaiian Ti

ARAUCARIA heterophylla
(ar-ow-KAR-ee-a het-er-o-FIL-a)   Norfolk Island Pine

BROMELIACEAE
(bro-mell-ee-AY-see-ee) most genera
and species   Bromeliads

CROSSANDRA infundibuliformis
(kross-AN-drah in-fun-di-buel-i-
FOR-mis)   Firecracker Flower

CHLOROPHYTUM comosum
(klo-ro-FI-tum ko-MOS-um)   Spider Plant

MIMOSA pudica
(mi-MO-sa PEW-di-ka)   Sensitive Plant

HOYA carnosa
(HOY-a kar-NOS-a)   Wax Plant

SEDUM morganianum
(SEE-dum mor-gan-ee-AN-um)   Burro's Tail

SENECIO macroglossus variegatus (sen-EK-ee-o mak-ro-GLOS-us var-ee-eh-GAHT-us)	Wax Ivy
SENECIO rowleyanus (sen-EK-ee-o row-lay-AN-us)	String of Pearls
SENECIO mikanioides (sen-EK-ee-o mik-an-ee-oy-dees)	German Ivy
LITHOPS (LIE-thops)	Living Stones
GRAPTOPETALUM paraguayense (grap-to-pet-AL-um par-a-GUAY-ens)	Ghost Plant
ZEBRINA pendula (ze-BREEN-a PEN-doo-la)	Wandering Jew
DIPLADENIA sanderi (dip-la-DEEN-ee-a SAN-der-eye)	Rose Dipladenia
ALSOPHILA cooperi (al-SOF-i-la KOO-per-eye)	Australia Tree Fern
EUPHORBIA lactea (you-FOR-bee-a lak-TAY-a)	Candelabra Cactus
EUPHORBIA lactea cristata (you-FOR-bee-a lak-TAY-a kris-TAH-ta)	Frilled Fan
EUPHORBIA submammillaris (you-FOR-bee-a sub-mam-il-AR-is)	
GIBASIS geniculata (ji-BAS-is jen-i-koo-LAHT-a)	Tahitian Bridal Veil

GROUP C   150-250 foot candles

Place plants in or very close to an unobstructed east, west or south window in the winter months. If the light intensity is too low, plants with a red, purple or yellow pigment in the leaves will become green and flowering plants will stretch and be slow to flower.

SAXIFRAGA sarmentosa
(sax-i-FRAG-a sar-men-TOS-a)   Strawberry Begonia

EUONYMUS japonicus medio-pictus
(you-OHN-im-us ya-PON-i-kus ME-di-
o-PIKT-us)   Goldspot Euonymus

ARDISIA crispa
(ar-DEES-ee-a KRIS-pa)   Coral Berry

GYNURA sarmentosa
(ji-NOOR-a sar-men-TOS-a)   Trailing Velvet

IRESINE
(eye-reh-SEE-nee)   e.g. Bloodleaf

FATSIA japonica
(FAHT-see-a ya-PON-i-ka)   Japanese Aralia

ASPARAGUS sprengeri
(as-PAR-a-gus SPRENG-er-eye)   Asparagus Fern

ASPARAGUS plumosa
(as-PAR-a-gus ploo-MOS-a)   Asparagus Fern

ASPARAGUS meyerii
(as-PAR-a-gus MY-er-eye)   Asparagus Fern

PORTULACARIA afra
(port-oo-la-KAR-ee-a AF-ra)   Elephant Jade

KLEINIA gomphophylla
(KLY-nee-a go-mo-FIL-a)   Gooseberry

DRACAENA angustifolia honoriae
(dra-SEE-na an-gust-i-FOL-ee-a
on-OR-ee-eye)   Ivory Margined

POLYSCIAS fruticosa
(po-LISS-ee-as froot-i-KOS-a)   Ming Aralia

POLYSCIAS balfouriana
(po-LISS-ee-as bal-four-ee-AHN-a)   Balfour Aralia

YUCCA elephantipes
(YUKK-a el-e-fan-TIP-es)   Yucca Cane

EUPHORBIA splendens (you-FOR-bee-a SPLEN-denz)	Crown of Thorns
COLEUS blumei (KOL-eh-us BLOOM-eye)	Painted Nettle
CLIVIA miniata grandiflora (KLI-vee-a min-ee-AY-ta grand-i-FLOR-a)	Kafir Lily
CACTACEAE (kak-TAY-see-ee) most species	Cactus
ALOE vera chinensis (AL-oh VE-ra kin-EN-sis)	Indian Medicine Plant
HIPPEASTRUM 'Leopoldii' (hip-ee-AHST-rum lee-o-POLD-eye)	Amaryllis
HIBISCUS rosa sinensis (hi-BIS-kus RO-sa si-NEN-sis) most varieties	Chinese Rose
LITHOPS (LIE-thops)	Living Stone
PASSIFLORA caerulea (pass-i-FLOR-a seh-RU-lee-a)	Passion Flower

Chapter 5
Bugs and Diseases

Fungus Gnats

I would like to ask about some Parsley that I would like to bring in. I know that fungus gnats have come into the house on other plants and I want to make sure that this Parsley is not infested with these fungus gnats or any other insects.

Probably the safest thing that you can use to control fungus gnats is diazinon granules. (There is a liquid concentrate of diazinon used in spray solutions, but it contains an emulsifier called xylene which is toxic to the roots of many plants when used as a soil drench.) The granules can be used outdoors or on potted plants to control many insects that attack root systems. Sprinkle the diazinon on the surface of the soil at about the same rate as you would put salt or pepper on your steak. Each time you water, some of the diazinon will dissolve, penetrate the soil and kill the fungus gnat larvae and any other soil insects that are in the pot.

Can I eat the Parsley right away?

Yes. Diazinon is recommended for use on edible crops. Just be certain that you follow the directions carefully. Is the Parsley growing in the garden at present?

No. I started it earlier in the spring in little plastic cups and I have them lined up in quart baskets. I would like to put them in larger pots and carry them over in the house all winter long so that I can have fresh Parsley for cooking.

This shouldn't be difficult to do. But remember that Parsley is a high light plant, so you are going to need a really bright window during the winter months. It also likes cool temperatures, even down to 5° to 10° C. In fact, Parsley will take a lot of frost if you leave it outdoors. So a cool, sunny window is the best place for it. Parsley also develops a large tap root, so you should choose pots that provide the greatest depth.

Fungus gnats are pesky little insects that have three life stages. The flying stage is a slender black fly similar to a fruit fly. The fly lays eggs on the surface of the soil. These hatch into larvae which eventually become the flying adults. The larva is the worm-like insect about 0.5 mm long, white and almost transparent, with a black head.

The larvae not only feed on organic matter in the soil, but they will also feed on the root system. Should they eat through the root where it originates near the stem, all of that portion cut off dies, rots, and causes all sorts of growth and disease problems.

Diazinon applied to the surface of the soil only takes care of the larva stage. You must also destroy the fungus gnat fly to break the life cycle of the insect. Otherwise, the fly lays eggs and by this time the diazinon may have been washed down through the soil and is no longer effective. The eggs then hatch into larvae.

To control the flying stage you can use a new spray insecticide with the active ingredient of resmethrin which is specific against fungus-gnat flies. Resmethrin is sold under many brand names as an indoor plant aerosol insecticide (check the active ingredients printed on all insecticide containers). Simply spray the plant whenever adult flies are seen. Another method is to put the plant that you want to clean up in a plastic bag. Spray short bursts of the resmethrin into the bag. Then close the bag for about two hours and keep the plant out of the sun.

Whiteflies

I have whiteflies. What can I do to get rid of them?

The whitefly is a very persistent insect. However, it can be controlled. Are the plants indoors or out?

They are outdoors now but I want to bring some of them indoors.

Some insecticides effective against whitefly cannot be used on food plants. Are they edible plants or ornamental?

Ornamental. One is Fuchsia.

It is easier to control the whitefly before bringing the plant indoors. Three insecticides are recommended—endosulfon, malathion and methoxychlor. These are the generic names. They are the active ingredients of many ornamental plant sprays, and are suitable for edible crops. Acephate, a systemic insecticide, is also recommended to control whitefly on ornamentals.

   You should start your control program about mid-August and repeat weekly until four sprays have been applied. Then your plants should be clean of the infestation and ready to move in well before any hard frost. Another excellent method of controlling whiteflies is with Vapona No-Pest Strips. Put the plant and the container in a plastic cleaner's bag, lay a Vapona No-Pest Strip on the soil, and close the bag. Leave the plant in the bag for about twelve hours, out of the sun so it doesn't get blistering hot inside. Repeat this every week for four weeks. This method will also work very well indoors.

Many ornamental and vegetable garden plants are host to the whitefly. The adults are about 2 mm long. They may remain undiscovered until the plant is disturbed and then, if the infestation is really bad, they fly out like a miniature snowstorm. The insect has a four-stage life cycle. The adult lays eggs that are pale yellow at first but turn grey before hatching in five to seven days, usually on the underside of leaves. The small nymphs or crawlers move on the leaf for one or two days and then stay in one place to feed. The nymphs develop fully in two weeks at normal temperatures. They then change into the slightly larger and thicker immobile, or pupa. The flying stage of the whitefly emerges from the pupa in about ten days. The complete life cycle takes about four weeks.

   Whitefly in the nymph or crawler stage is a sap-sucker and if uncontrolled can cause withering of the leaves. The insect also secretes what entomologists call honeydew, a substance which promotes the growth of disfiguring Sooty Mould fungus.

   The only stage that is readily controlled with insecticides is the flying stage. This is why it is necessary to apply insecticide at least four times approximately a week apart. As each stage of adults hatches out, the insecticide kills it and prevents further egg-laying. In this way the life-cycle is blocked and a cleanup of the infestation is possible.

Bacterial Stem and Leaf Rot

I have a Dieffenbachia that is in real trouble. It just won't grow. Every time a new leaf comes along the bottom one drops off. The leaves are kind of withered.

Dieffenbachia are subject to a systemic disease that destroys the leaves. Even the centre portion of the leaf will begin to turn brown and soft, and eventually the whole leaf dies. Is this the problem?

That is it exactly.

I'm afraid there is no way of controlling this disease under household conditions. It is right in the tissue of the plant and is eventually transmitted by growth processes throughout the plant. Under greenhouse conditions we can control this disease with antibiotics, but in a home situation there is no way that you can clean it up. All that you can really do is go to a reliable greenhouse and start again with a fresh, clean plant. Even if you took a cutting from your present plant it would likely have the disease.

With bacterial stem rot (Erwinia chrysanthemi), stem lesions are water-soaked, soft and greyish at first, later becoming tan to pale brown and sunken. There is a clear demarcation between diseased and healthy tissues. Lesions may occur beneath the soil. Leaves on infected plants are reduced in size and pale yellow. Leaf spotting may also occur; spots are small, water-soaked, pale brown and surrounded by a diffused yellow margin. The spots may enlarge, becoming irregular and sunken with light tan centres and darker brown borders.* The same disease attacks Philodendron selloum, Philodendron pandurata, and Syngonium podophyllum, appearing as mushy, water-soaked areas of the leaf and petiole.

---

*Ref. McFadden, Lorne A. 1961. *Bacterial stem and leaf rot of Dieffenbachia in Florida*. Phytopathology 51: 663-668; Munnecke, Donald E. 1960. *Bacterial stem rot of Dieffenbachia*. Phytopathology 50: 696-700.

Botrytis

I've noticed a few brown sections on the base of the leaves of my Poinsettia. When I examined them carefully I saw a sort of fine white material. They weren't flying away or moving and they are not mealy bugs because they are not furry, but they do look a little bit like an insect.

Is the white material on a stem about 2 mm long with many of the stems clustered together? Do parts of the leaves turn brown and mushy?

Yes.

What you are seeing is not an insect but the spore stage of a fungus disease called Botrytis. I recommend that you carefully take those leaves off and discard them right away.

I did that at first but now I notice that the same thing is appearing on the upper leaves and seems to be spreading throughout the plant.

Are you misting the plant at all?

No, it is pretty humid in there. I would estimate at least seventy per cent.

High humidity encourages Botrytis to spread. Also, the dust-like spores that you see on the tiny stems of the mature stage of Botrytis will move on air currents and attack any susceptible plant. The best fungicide to control it is benomyl, which is systemic in action with a residual effect of two to four weeks. (Systemic fungicides are absorbed into the tissue of the plant and continue to work over a period of time). You can also use Funginex or captan, which are contact fungicides. All these are safe to apply in the house.

Botrytis cinerea (Grey Mould) is characterized by the rotting or breaking down of tissue on young leaves or petals. If it attacks the bracts (coloured leaves) of a Poinsettia, the infected parts will turn a purplish colour. The tissue eventually turns brown and dries up. In the presence of lots of moisture it will be soggy and rotten. Out of this diseased tissue the Botrytis will develop a tiny 2 mm stem bearing a cluster of dust-like spores. If disturbed at this point the spores will fly into the air like the seeds of a dandelion, drifting to susceptible hosts to carry on their parasitic life.

Botrytis can cause damping off (rotting of the stem at the soil line) of seedlings, stem cankers, leaf and petal spots and tuber rots. It will attack vegetables, fruit and many flowers. Soft mushy spots on Strawberries are usually symptomatic of Botrytis, as are small black spots on Petunias that eventually grow and engulf the whole flower. Black petals at the centre of Geranium flowers are often caused by Botrytis.

On Baby's Tears Botrytis attacks the leaves and stems, turning them soft and brown. Because of the dense growth on Baby's Tears the disease can spread quickly.

There is always greater danger of Botrytis infection when dead leaf tissue is present underneath the growing leaves where the moisture level is high. Botrytis generally requires one hundred per cent humidity at the site of the infection and germinates best at temperatures around 14°C or lower. Spores require about six to eight hours to germinate in the presence of moisture and cool temperatures.

While the fungicides recommended will help to control the disease, the first line of defense is to control the environment. Avoid physical injury to the plants, create air circulation and introduce heat to lower the humidity. Watering should be done early in the morning, preferably on a bright day, and the plant placed where there is lots of air movement around it until the leaves dry. The shorter the period that the leaves are moist the less likely that Botrytis will start. Temperatures above 14°C do not favour the germination of Botrytis spores. In addition, any dead tissue on plant material should be removed.

Scale

I hope you can help me with a problem with my Orange tree because I don't want a second catastrophe. The first one died because I bought it from a supermarket and didn't know it was laden with some type of mite. I bought another one this summer and put it on the balcony and it was coming along beautifully. Suddenly it was covered with what a neighbour said was scale. I have never heard of scale. I understand it is an insect. How can I control it?

It is indeed an insect. Nature has provided natural predators of scale: the tiny wasp and the lady beetle or lady bug. These, however, are not usually found inside our homes, and hence we have to use other measures of control.

You must understand a little of the life cycle of a particular insect in order to control it. The actual scale is like armour: it protects the life within from insecticides (although the natural predators can penetrate this). There is, however, a crawler stage that you can control with repeated sprays of either malathion or diazinon. If you can put the plant outdoors so there is free movement of air around the plant and yourself while you are spraying, you can use a systemic insecticide such as oxydemeton-methyl, dimethoate 23%, or acephate. These sprays should be applied about every two weeks for at least three applications.

But how is it that the scale can appear so suddenly?

It is not really that they appeared suddenly but that suddenly you saw them. The critical thing is to know what to look for and to keep constant vigilance in order to discover whether or not insects are at work.

Scale insects fall broadly into two groups: armoured, or hard-scale insects, and soft-scale insects. Armoured scale live beneath an outer shell of moulted skins and waxy secretions. The soft-scale shell is an integral part of the scale, like the shell of the turtle, and though called soft, it is often as hard as armoured scale. The scales vary somewhat in size and shape. Colours range from a soft beige through brown to black depending on type and maturity. They adhere closely to the outer skin of the leaf and are 2 to 5 mm in diameter.

Because scales are very small, by the time the infestation is noted the population is usually so great that the plant is disfigured. The soft scale also excretes honey dew, which encourages the growth of a fungus called Sooty Mould. It is often this sticky excretia and the mould that alerts people to the presence of the insect.

Eggs (up to as many as two thousand) are produced beneath a female shell, and hatch into translucent crawlers. This is the only stage not covered by a relatively hard covering. Crawlers move over new foliage to locate feeding sites on or near veins on the underside of leaves. This stage is practically invisible to the naked eye. When the crawlers locate a suitable site they insert their mouth parts, which can uncoil to six or seven times the length of the insect's body, and reach deep into the plant tissue to suck juices and reduce plant vitality. Foliage pales, needles and leaves drop prematurely. Heavy infestations may kill branches, sometimes entire plants. The crawler matures, sometimes shedding as many as two or three outer skins which remain to form a part of the final shell.

If you have what appears to be scale you can check to see if it is living by using the point of a knife. If it is firmly attached to the plant as opposed to being a part of the plant (many plants have a brown flecking on the surface of the stems which could be mistaken for scale) and if the top cover pops off revealing a yellow-orangish plump mass attached to the leaf surface, consider the scale alive. However, if no live nymph is present it may simply mean that all that remains under the shell are eggs ready to hatch into another generation of crawlers. You must use at least a ten-power hand lense to detect the miniature jellybean-like eggs beneath the empty female shell.

The presence of the scale then, whether or not anything live is found underneath, means that you should begin a control program. Host plants for scale include all types of Ficus, Citrus, Ferns and Cacti. Some of these plants may have a toxic reaction to some of the insecticides listed above so you should use the insecticide experimentally on two or three fronds or branches before an overall spraying. The effectiveness of non-systemic insecticides (e.g. malathion and diazinon) may be greatly increased by substituting two thirds of the water used in making up the spray solution with rubbing alcohol or one half with ethonol. Again, use experimentally on part of the plant and wait forty-eight to seventy-two hours for a possible toxic reaction.

The scales can also be removed manually with a Q-tip and alcohol, but bear in mind that you may not clear up all the eggs this way, and you certainly would not remove the near-invisible crawlers.

Aphids and Spider Mites

My Ivy plants, brought in from outside, have a tiny, pale-green insect about the size of a pinhead. You can see them crawl on little legs.

Then this is a type of aphid.

I have sprayed the plant twice and I still have them.

Then you are going to have to switch insecticides. Switching brand names may not help at all. What you must check is the active ingredient listed on the container. Then look for another insecticide recommended for the control of aphids with a different active ingredient. An insecticide may work on one type of aphid and not on another, or, if applied continuously, successive generations of the insect may develop immunity to a certain type of spray.

Is it the aphids that make the leaves deformed?

Yes, they do. Aphids generally feed off the soft growing tips of the plant and the injury done while the leaf is young is greatly exaggerated as it matures. They can actually take sections out of them and twist stems, giving a very crippled appearance to the leaf and stem. A large population will really distort and stunt plant growth. If your Ivy has been outdoors you must also realize that it acts as a host for spider mite. Check the underside of the foliage for these tiny insects about a quarter of the size of the aphid. Usually the one present on Ivy is grey in colour with two tiny black spots on the abdomen, although you certainly could not see these without a ten-power magnifying glass.

Do these insects make little pin-prick bumps?

The spider mite feeds by scratching the surface of the leaf which then bleeds sap. The insect feeds on this sap. If the leaf heals it will leave scar tissue on the surface that grows along with the leaf. More characteristically, however, mites seen on the underside of the leaves produce a greyish or yellowish speckling which is especially prominent when viewing the upper leaf surface. With a severe infestation a fine webbing will appear and the affected leaves become dry and drop off.

Aphids are plump, soft-bodied insects which normally feed on young developing leaves and stems or the opening buds and petals of flowers, causing malformed, twisted plant growth and, in severe cases, stunting. The body colour of the live aphid camouflages it on the host plant. Often the first things that you notice are the white shed skins on the leaves, stem or flowers.

Multiplication rates of aphids, when uncontrolled, are enormous. When the populations become overcrowded, winged forms may be produced which rapidly spread to other plants in your garden or home.

Aphids also excrete a sticky honey dew which coats the infested foliage and encourages the growth of the unsightly black Sooty Mould. Usually control of this insect is achieved by using the proper insecticide only once, but if this does not work quickly then change to an insecticide with a different active ingredient. Diazinon, endosulfon, oxydemeton-methyl, primicarb, resmethrin and acephate are recommended against aphids. Aphids are frequently found on Aphelandra (Zebra Plant), Brassaia (Schefflera), Gynura (Purple Passion), Hibiscus, Hoya, Dieffenbachia, Asparagus Fern, Iresine (Bloodleaf) and Fuchsia.

Spider mites vary in size from 0.25 to 1 mm and in colour from translucent pale yellow and pale green to dark green and red. Under a ten to fourteen power magnifying glass any community of spider mites can be seen to consist of eggs, empty egg shells, six-legged larvae, nymphs and adults plus the shed skins of adults. On a compatible host in dry conditions above 23°C they multiply at an astronomical rate. When their numbers increase, mites congregate in an orange-coloured mass at the apex of the plant leaves. Individual mites then drop on silken threads forming a rope of living mites. A heavy population of spider mites on the opening buds of a flower can actually web over the flower and prevent it from opening.

They spread to other plants on air currents or on clothes or your hands as you care for plant material. High-rise office buildings with central air conditioning and ducts running from one floor to another can carry insects from one plant throughout an entire building.

Each spider mite has a pair of needle-like stylets, or teeth, which rupture the cells of the host leaf tissue. The mouth of the spider mite then is pushed into the torn cells to draw cell sap. It is this feeding action which causes the fine flecking or stippling of the foliage. Under heavy populations of these mites sometimes the entire leaf turns yellow or bronze.

It is important to realize that most miticides (insecticides designed specifically to control mites) kill only the adult mite. It takes about twenty to twenty-eight days for the mite to go from the egg stage to the adult. It is therefore necessary to use the insecticide about once every five to seven days for four applications. If the insecticide is not providing control, change to another active ingredient. Mite populations quickly develop resistance to many miticides.

One method that I have found to control spider mite is to place the plant in a plastic bag along with a Vapona No-Pest Strip or part of a strip if the plant is small. Probably 3 cm of strip for every 25 cm of bag is a good rule of thumb. Seal the bag for about eight hours overnight. Repeat this weekly for three or four fumigations. For a large plant over one metre tall a plastic cleaner's bag may be used. Most plant stores also have plastic tubing that they use to pack plants in in the winter time and this can be purchased for larger plants.

Insecticide labels will indicate whether or not a product is considered effective against mites (insecticides containing decofol, ethion, oxydemeton-methyl, tetradefon, malathion, acephate, resmethrin or dichlorvos). Plants that frequently host mites are Asparagus Fern, Brassaia (Schefflera), Codiaeum (Croton), Chamaedorea (Palms), Cordyline, Dieffenbachia, Dracaena and Hedera (Ivy).

Be sure to read all of the label on any insecticide or chemical, and, when using an insecticide on a plant for the first time, always spray or treat just a few of the leaves and wait for forty-eight hours to see if there is a toxic effect. As a precaution, use rubber gloves when handling any insecticide.

Mealy Bugs

I have a beautiful Shrimp Plant and it seems to be infested with a fluffy white insect.

Does it look like a piece of fuzzy, white oatmeal?

Yes, and there are several of them clustered together.

The common name of that insect is mealy bug. The problem with controlling it is that the white fuzzy exterior is very waxy and acts as a protection against insecticides and predators. If there are not too many of them on the plant you can remove them with a Q-tip soaked in alcohol. Contact insecticides such as diazinon and malathion applied every two weeks for three to four applications may control the insect, although they may not penetrate the outer waxy coating (their effectiveness can be increased considerably by using the alcohol dilution recommended on page 66). If you can put your plants outdoors while you are spraying you can use dimethoate 23% or oxydemeton-methyl, which are both systemic insecticides. Spray a leaf or two at first and wait for forty-eight hours to see if there is any toxic effect.

There are several types of mealy bugs that attack ornamental plants, but the most common one is the long-tailed type (Pseudococcus longispinus). They may infest all plant parts — roots, stems, twigs, leaves and even flowers and fruit. The adult female is about 3 mm long. The insect multiplies rapidly and all stages are usually found in clusters on the host plant at the same time. Ants sometimes aid in carrying mealy bugs from plant to plant. Injury to the host plant is caused by loss of sap which results in discoloured foliage, leaf deformation, and the eventual death of the affected parts.

In addition to Beloperone (Shrimp Plant), common plants that should be watched closely for mealy bugs are Palms, Peperomia, Dieffenbachia, Philodendron, Syngonium, Aphelandra, Gynura, Asparagus, Dracaena, Maranta, Dizygotheca, Cactus and many succulents.

Chapter 6
Flowering

Azaleas

I have an Azalea which was given to me in May. When the blooms finally stopped, I planted it in the garden, in the pot, where it seems to be doing fine. What do I do now to get it to reflower?

Getting an Azalea to put on new growth from down below where the old flowers were is mainly a matter of controlling the temperature. Most forcing types of Azaleas, which is the type that you have, will set buds on new growth after eight weeks of temperatures averaging 16°C. This is about normal summer weather, so you can expect to have buds set by late July or early August. In order to prepare the flower buds to open during the winter the plant needs a further cool treatment for approximately six weeks. Buds should continue to develop during this period but you must make sure that the plant does not receive frost. Temperatures should range from above freezing to 6°C. This conditioning period is essential for flower development, and can take place outdoors until there is danger of frost.

Should I then put the plant in a cold part of the basement?

Yes, but they require some light even at these low temperatures. A forty-watt bulb hung 30 cm above the plant provides sufficient light to bring it through this conditioning period.

If you have received your Azalea at Christmas or late in the winter, new growth should begin to appear three to four weeks after the flowers are finished. It would be advisable to pinch out or remove half of this new growth when it has become 8 to 10 cm long. Do not, however, pinch down into the hard original wood. The plant can be shaped in this manner and the number of blooms increased by increasing the number of branches (they will branch out where the leaves join the stem below where the tip of the plant has been removed). Discontinue all pinching in May. If the plant has put on a lot of growth it may need to be up-potted. I would use a straight, coarse peat and increase the pot size by about 5 cm. The pot and plant can then be plunged into the garden in a shady spot. Take care that it does not dry out during the summer months.

Azaleas require an acidic soil. Should you notice the leaves turning yellow but the veins of the leaves remaining green, it is a sign that they need fertilizing with iron. A readily available source of this and other trace elements is a product called Ortho Greenall. Simply follow the directions on the container. If the plant and pot are subjected to rain during the summer, fertilize once a month with a water-soluble 20-20-20 fertilizer or use controlled-release fertilizer pellets when the plant is outdoors (see Chapter 3). If the temperature during the cool conditioning period rises up to over 12°C it will cause uneven development of the buds so it is important to try to keep the temperature uniform between 0° and 6°C.

Amaryllis Bulbs

I have a couple of Amaryllis that I have kept around from last year. They were out on the balcony and had a lot of leaves. I brought them in and they have been dry ever since November. In other years, the minute I give them one drop of water they put up new leaves but I get no flowers. When you buy them in the store they are dry and have flowerbuds coming up. What can I do?

Amaryllis, like many other flower bulbs, require a cold dormant period to initiate buds. Take the plant in mid-September, lift it out of the pot, shake off the soil and allow the leaves and the plant to completely dry up. Then clean off the dead leaves and put the bulb in the refrigerator for about six to eight weeks. This should accomplish the dormancy requirement and ready the bulb for flowering. Replant the bulb into potting soil in mid-November, water it and it should be in bloom again by Christmas time.

Well, I put my plants in a cold sunroom. Shouldn't this have worked?

It is not likely that the temperature in your sunroom was low enough. It should be from 2° to 5°C to accomplish the change in the bulb.

To successfully reflower an Amaryllis, it is necessary to do several things. After they have completed their flowering keep the plant growing actively. During the flowering period the plant is using most of its plant food stored in the bulb to produce the flower. Once the flowering process is over this stored plant food must be renewed. This is done by keeping the plant actively growing so that the leaves regenerate the bulb. You must keep up normal watering practices and the occasional fertilizing, maybe once every month, with a water-soluble 20-20-20 fertilizer. Keep the plant in a bright sunny room.

Once the danger of frost is past, the bulb and the pot can be plunged into a flowerbed outdoors with the bulb about 2 cm below the soil level. It should continue to grow all summer. Don't be concerned when the first frost in the fall freezes the leaves down. The longer you can leave it outdoors the better, as long as the bulb itself does not get severe frost. To prevent this, cover the bulb with another 5 cm of soil until some time in late October or mid-November. With this dormancy period the bulb should have received six to eight weeks of temperatures near the freezing point but not actually freezing. Make sure that the bulb does not receive severe enough frost (-5°C) to penetrate the 5 cm of soil and actually harm the bulb. At this point the Amaryllis can be brought indoors, usually without repotting. It should start to flower in a very short time. If you are successful the original bulb will produce side shoots which may necessitate up-potting when they begin to fill the pot. The offshoots can also be separated from the parent bulb and potted individually at the end of the flowering period. They take three to five years of active growth to reach flowering size.

If the cool period cannot be completed outdoors, due to low outdoor temperatures, remove the dormant bulb from the soil, clean it with a brush and complete the dormancy period in your refrigerator. To start them up again, simply plant them in a pot that is at least 5 cm larger than the bulb. Use a well-drained potting soil, and leave the tip of the bulb just above the soil. Water, and place in light at room temperature. The Amaryllis should be in beautiful flower in just a few weeks.

Hoya

I have a Hoya growing in a 15 cm pot. I have had it for about three years. It looks very healthy but it never blooms. How do you get a Hoya to flower?

Hoya requires a lot of light to flower. In the winter this is often a problem. They should be in a window where they receive direct sunlight. Do you have such a spot?

No. The house has a big overhang.

Do you have an east, west or south window?

It is in an east window.

If that is the best you can do, and of course you have to remember that the overhang cuts down the light intensity, then you should try and correct the other factors which influence blooming and it may flower for you. In the late fall and winter months you should withhold water to harden and ripen the wood. This means allowing the plant to wilt slightly between waterings. Then water thoroughly. It will also require a lowering of the temperature during the same period to 10° to 12°C.

What about fertilizing?

Once the bud has set, resume normal watering practices and when the flowering period is over the plant will again begin to put on new growth. This is the time when it should be fertilized, possibly once a month during the warm, bright summer months.

Hoya, like many other flowering plants, react favourably to the hardship of withholding water to ripen the wood and initiate flowering. The Hoya flower is produced in clusters, similar to the Verbena or Geranium, and it receives its common name of Wax Plant from the fact that the flowers are very waxy and firm in appearance. The leaves of many Hoya are also heavy, waxy and hold their shape even when under severe water stress. However, they do become softer to the touch and slightly wrinkled, enabling you to detect wilting. Do not remove the spurs that remain after the flowering is complete. The Hoya will flower again on these same spurs.

Hoya may be trained on a pole or tied to a wire that has been formed into a circle and fastened to the pot or inserted into the soil (this trained growth should also receive direct sunlight, otherwise flowering will not occur). Branching can be encouraged during the growth period by pinching (removing) 5 cm of the growing tips. The pinched-out cutting can be rooted (see Chapter 8).

Cyclamen

I have a Cyclamen and the flowers are finished. Is there any trick to putting it to rest and getting it to bloom again?

How long has it presently been in bloom?

About a month.

The blooming period should have been longer than that. Under correct conditions they will flower for six to eight months. The limiting factor in getting this long blooming period is usually the high temperatures in our homes. Under temperatures of around 20° to 21°C and particularly with inadequate light the blooms die back and the leaves turn yellow very quickly. New buds are not formed. They do best at a temperature of about 12°C with bright diffused light.

I have a very cool west window. Would that be all right?

That would be excellent. When you come to the warm summer months of June, July, August and into September, begin to dry out the plant by withholding water, letting the leaves droop and finally dry up. By this time the plant should have formed a corm (similar to a bulb) clearly visible on the surface of the soil. You are inducing the required dormant period by withholding water and letting it die back. Begin to water again in the cool weather of late September. Leaves will form again, buds will set and it should reflower throughout the winter and spring months.

In August a good customer of ours brought into the greenhouse the strangest Cyclamen I have ever seen. She told me that it was still in the 15 cm clay pot that it had been growing in when she received it. It was given to her when her daughter was in grade eight. Her daughter had subsequently completed her Masters degree at university and had worked for a year, so she was certain her Cyclamen was fifteen years old. It had developed a large brown corm that was about 10 cm across rising 5 cm above the soil level. Growing up from the corm were six or seven gnarled, whiskery stems about 10 cm long. The whiskers were the dried-up remains of years of leaves that had died back. The plant looked like an arthritic octopus upside down. At the top of each stem was a tuft of white leaves and a few buds, for the Cyclamen was presently in its dry rest period, although a later examination revealed a number of new, white roots forming.

I had never seen a fifteen-year old Cyclamen. Our customer wanted it repotted but I demurred at the thought of repotting a family heirloom. If I did something wrong and it turned up its toes and died, it would cause, I was sure, a crisis of major proportions in the family.

The Cyclamen had never been repotted and successive years of root systems and maybe the odd bump or two had cracked the clay pot until it was almost in half, but still the plant grew on. She told me that it was covered with a mass of leaves and bloom from October to late spring. The plant held a place of honour in the living room, right next to the centre of a large picture window. It sat on an old tea wagon over the hot air register. As we discussed this position, we realized that the tea wagon deflected the heat sideways so that it did not actually strike the Cyclamen. The large expanse of window would not only provide direct light, but would cool the air, causing a down-draft of cooler air which probably swept gently over the Cyclamen. It had its own ideal micro-climate.

I smashed off the remains of the old pot with a hammer, and up-potted it two sizes, disturbing the roots as little as I could. I left it at the same depth as it was in its original pot and prayed that everything would go well with this fine old specimen.

Poinsettias

I have a question about a Poinsettia. Mine is three years old and it is very big. It has about eighteen buds on it but everything seems to be sort of stationary.

Are the bracts turning red yet?

They are just a little bit pink but they are very tiny.

And is there a little pea-like flower or bud in the centre?

Yes.

Then the plant has set buds and bracts and is attempting to develop them fully. Obviously now that it is early December the bracts are not going to be fully developed by Christmas. The problem is that in the home all the growth processes are slowed down due to lower light. All you can do is compensate by starting the short-day treatment earlier, and giving the plant the best possible light exposure.

Reflowering a Poinsettia is a fun thing to do. Often the plant has been received as a gift and there is an emotional attachment, not only to the plant, but to the giver and the occasion. There is no reason why the same plant cannot be reflowered again and again.

When the plant is first brought into your home, always make sure that the drainage holes in the pot are not blocked by decorative wrapping or foil. If they are, puncture this wrapping or remove it when watering so that the drainage water flows freely from the pot.

Correct light and temperature will increase the longevity of the flowering stage. At normal room temperature the colour of the bract will fade rather rapidly. If, however, you can put it in about 15°C, the colour will remain more intense for a longer time. Bright light will also increase the life of the plant.

If the lower leaves begin to yellow and drop off quickly after you receive the plant, then look to either incorrect watering practices or poor placement, where it may look beautiful but receives very little light. Place the plant where you can enjoy it fully when you are in the room, but whenever possible during daylight hours put it close to a window. No fertilizer is required at this point because there is no new growth. If these minimum requirements are met the bracts should last for several months.

The first week in April grit your teeth and cut all branches back to within 15 to 20 cm of the top of the pot. Do not be concerned about the flow of latex sap from the cut stem. It will quickly cease. Decrease the frequency of watering for the next four or five weeks because you have removed a great deal of the leaf area which transpired water.

The plant will end up being larger than it was the year before, so it would be advisable the first week in June to up-pot it one or two pot sizes using well-drained potting soil. At the same time pinch out the top 5 cm of each stem that has resulted from the cutting back. This will cause further branching and make a more shapely plant. Water thoroughly and plunge this pot up to the rim in a flowerbed where the plant will receive at least four hours' sunlight sometime during the day. You will have to check its water requirements for the next three or four weeks until it roots through the drainage hole into the flowerbed.

Repeat the pinching process on all the subsequent branches about mid-July and at the same time turn the pot so that you sever the roots that have gone out into the flowerbed. This root pruning is essential once or twice during the summer, otherwise the plant will go into severe shock when removed from the garden in the fall, just at the critical time of budset. Again, check water requirements for the few weeks following this root pruning.

In a greenhouse situation where there is lots of light, the Poinsettia will begin to initiate buds about the first week in October. If the temperature and all other factors are correct the buds and bracts will be at full maturity in the first or second week in December. However, in the home the growth processes that bring about maturity are so slowed by lack of light that the budset process must be begun artificially earlier than October first.

The Poinsettia is photoperiodic and must have short days and long nights in order to set bud and bloom. I would recommend that you begin manipulating the day length around September first by making sure that the plant receives full exposure to available sunlight for about eleven hours and uninterrupted darkness for thirteen. I emphasize unbroken darkness because many commercial growers have found that street lights near their greenhouse where they are growing Poinsettias can often delay or prevent blooming. This treatment can be begun while the Poinsettia is still in the garden by putting a cardboard box over the plant at about 5 p.m. and removing it around 8 a.m. (natural day length at this time is not short enough to initiate budset). This is preferable to bringing the plant inside because the light intensity outdoors is almost always better, resulting in a sharper response to shortened day length. This method will work until night temperatures outdoors begin to dip below 8°C (remember that the cardboard carton will have an insulating effect and maintain a five degree higher temperature than prevailing night temperatures). When low temperatures dictate bringing the plant indoors, continue manipulating the day length by putting the plant in a closet or dark room at night until the tiny buds are the size of a pea and the bracts themselves are fully coloured and about 10 cm long and 3 cm wide. After this point, normal extensions of day length by room lighting are usually not sufficient to delay bract and flower development.

The same procedure may be duplicated the following year, except that the initial cutting back will have to be somewhat higher on the plant, probably 25 to 30 cm above the pot rim.

As the years go by the plant will develop a brown bark and heavy stem. You may then choose to simply withhold water and let the plant dry out and the leaves fall off when flowering is finished. This is the way Poinsettias used to be grown fifteen or twenty years ago. The mother plants were produced in California and grown to about one metre, then cut back and allowed to dry out. These dormant, dry stock plants were then shipped to eastern growers. Replanting in containers plus watering produced new growth and summer cuttings for their Christmas Poinsettias.

You may do the same thing with a four or five year old plant by cutting the plant back when the blooms are finished, allowing the plant to dry out and defoliate, leaving it right in the pot. Once the leaves are all off it may be stored in the dark providing it is never watered. About July 15th bring it out into the light, plunge it in a flowerbed or put it on a patio (starting a new growth cycle much earlier will result in a larger plant requiring considerably more window space). Water thoroughly, mist the plant and cover it with clear plastic until green buds are visible. Be ready to repeat the process of setting the buds by manipulating day length the first week in September.

If your Poinsettia is placed for its summer holidays where it receives rain, you should fertilize at least once every month throughout the summer period with a water-soluble 20-20-20 fertilizer, or one application of controlled-release fertilizer capsules at the beginning of the summer (see Chapter 3).

The size and quality of the bracts will be greatly improved at the time you begin shortening the day length if you also thin out all the weak branches (up to a third or half of the branches that have formed). Simply cut them right off at the trunk and discard them. The remaining branches will produce a much better flower.

Citrus Trees

I have an Orange tree that was given to me about a year ago. It is now about 60 cm high and last year at this time it had about forty oranges on it. This year it is not producing any.

Is this the Calamondin Orange with the small fruit about the size of a ping-pong ball that has a very bitter taste?

Yes, it is.

All Citrus, including the Calamondin Orange, need a cool, almost dormant period during January, February and March. If the fruit is still on at this time, this will increase the juiciness and flavour of it. It will also ripen the wood and induce budset and flowering. The ideal situation is full light, preferably a southern exposure, and in temperatures down in the 10°C range. If you don't have such a situation in your home you may be able to achieve budset by putting it in a protected spot outdoors in April and May, bringing it indoors when frost is forecast. In the summer put them in a place where they are in bright shade. Leaves that are produced under full summer light will not make the transition into the low light of the home in the winter and will often drop off. It is critical after the tree has flowered and the tiny fruit has set that they receive even moisture. A drying out to the point of wilting at this point will cause the embryo fruit to abort.

Summer vacations outdoors in shaded locations for most house plants of tropical origin benefit the plants greatly, particularly if they are exposed to rain and protected from wind. The risk is that if there are long dry spells and you forget to water them, they will dry out to the point of permanent damage. Temperatures outdoors in summer are often even higher than they are indoors. This, plus greater air movement, increases the transpiration of water from the leaves and therefore the water requirements of the plants. Keep in mind, too, that most tropical plants are planted in soils that are very high in peat content. This is often difficult to wet once it has been thoroughly dried out, and may require a very long watering, almost a leaching, to get it wet again.

In high-rise apartments and homes that do not have nearby flower-beds, the absence of insects to pollinate the flowers can be a problem. With limited equipment you can do what the insects normally do. As the Citrus sets buds and flowers you can observe that the bud grows as a solid, bullet-shaped white bud, until one day five petals open up and spread their wings, releasing a delightful fragrance. As they curve away from the centre of the flower, the stamens develop and form a yellow tiara of anthers around the central pistil of the flower. You will know that the pollen is ripe when you are able to pick up some of it on a small water-colour paintbrush. Move it from the anther to the stigma (tip of the pistil). This will pollinate the bloom and set the fruit. It has the additional benefit of dispersing the sweet, heavy scent of the Citrus bloom.

When you move the plant to its summer location you should also consider pruning any wayward branches that destroy the symmetrical shape of the plant. The Citrus will grow very unevenly unless you do judicious pruning. The plant should grow actively during the spring and summer months and routine feeding once a month with a water-soluble 20-20-20 fertilizer will be necessary. If you find a fair number of white growing tips on the root system and the foliage is pale green you can step up the frequency of fertilizing. Where the plant is exposed to rain, one application after the first heavy rainfall of a controlled release 14-14-14 fertilizer will sustain growth all summer.

The bitter Calamondin Orange makes delightful marmalade. As the plant gets bigger you will, with luck, get a sufficient crop to produce this taste treat.

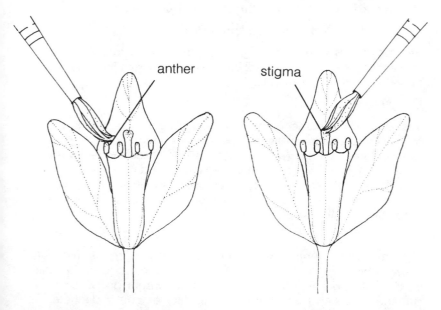

A cross-section of a Citrus flower illustrating how to pick up the mature pollen from the anthers at the tip of the stamen and place it on the stigma at the tip of the pistil.

Hibiscus

My question is about a bushy tree. The only name I have heard applied to it is "Chinese Rose." It has beautiful flowers on it each year.

It sounds like Hibiscus. Are the leaves oval, dark green and very shiny?

Yes.

And the flowers single?

No. Double.

Fine. There are both types of flowers, usually measuring 7 to 10 cm in size. Hibiscus make a delightful house plant in a bright south window. It is a tropical shrub used as an outdoor ornamental in the frost-free parts of the world. Recent hybridizing has generated larger, sometimes double blooms plus growth habits more suitable to indoor pot culture. They can be put outdoors in summer as long as you put them in shade. Hibiscus are a testy tropical that will really talk back to you if you dramatically change the light intensity the plant receives. If it goes from a high-light situation to a low-light situation when you move the plant indoors in the fall it will simply defoliate. The new hybrid varieties have better foliage retention under difficult low-light conditions. The flower life has also been extended to three to five days.

It is about 1.5 m high now. Can I prune it?

Yes, they do respond to pruning. Simply trim it down to the size and shape that you want it and it will branch out even from hard wood, provided it is receiving bright light.

Do you feed them?

Yes. During the summer months when they are growing rapidly they do respond to a regular application, maybe once a month, of a water-soluble fertilizer. This is particularly true if they are outdoors and receive rain. In the winter when the light is low and they are growing very little they should not be fed at all. Because they are a shrubby plant, they do not respond well to severe drying out. Even moisture, but not saturated soil, is ideal.

Gramma Reeves nursed a small Hibiscus in the greenhouse until it grew to be a bushy tree two metres high. Every once in a while it would outgrow its position and Gramma would go at it with the pruning sheers and lop off branches as thick as 3 cm in diameter. The Hibiscus would truculently sit there for a while and then as the sun increased in the spring it would send out new branches and a glorious crop of single red blooms. It became a symbol of her skill with plants and customers who knew her would always inquire about the state of the Hibiscus. It became a friend of many people. Each spring it brought forth its glorious crop of blooms that went on appearing well into late fall. The beautiful flowers opened and lasted only twenty-four to forty-eight hours. Like a note in a musical score, they had their moment of glory and then passed on quickly, making them all the more beautiful. When Gramma passed on in 1970, the Hibiscus followed shortly thereafter.

Chapter 7
Wintering

Geraniums

My question is on Geraniums. I have good luck with digging them up in the fall and hanging them up in the cellar, then putting them out again in the spring. Could I pot them when I dig them up in the fall and just let them go dry and die down?

Both storage techniques work reasonably well if you have a cool part of the basement that runs around 4° or 5°C. The problem is that most basements run almost as warm as the rest of the house so that the plant simply dehydrates during the winter. If the technique of digging the plants up in the fall, shaking off nearly all the soil and hanging them up has worked for you, there is no reason why you could not leave the soil on and pot them instead. At that time you should also cut them back by half. This will reduce the leaf area that transpires moisture and reduce dehydration of the plants generally. Water only once or twice during the winter months.

The reason that uprooting Geraniums and hanging them in the basement used to work was that our basements in the older homes were much cooler—just above freezing. At this low temperature the plants would not completely dehydrate.

Before you attempt to winter over Geraniums by this method you should check to see if you really do have a part of your basement which stays at no more that 4°C all winter long. Because you are keeping the plant dormant, a lot of light is not really required. If you do have a light basement you can run higher temperatures and keep the plants growing in a pot at a minimum rate. I would spray the plants with benomyl after they are cut back to destroy any fungus spores. Keeping the foliage dry all winter will also help prevent fungus damage.

In warm basements, or an apartment at 20° to 21°C, bare-root Geraniums are going to dehydrate quickly. You will have dead, dry sticks by the time next spring rolls around. You can, however, perpetuate those Geraniums by taking cuttings off them and growing these small plants in a bright window through the winter (see Chapter 8).

Tuberous Begonias

I have in the garden a beautiful Tuberous Begonia that is flowering right now. What is the procedure for keeping it over the winter?

Do you want to keep the plant growing or do you simply want to store it over the winter?

My main concern is to keep it to replant in my patio garden next year.

You may leave it outside then until the leaves are touched with light frost. It is critical, however, that you do not let the plant be subjected to heavy frost which could freeze the tuber as well. Dig the Begonia out before severe frost, shake off any excess soil and let the leaves and the tuber dry thoroughly. Once the leaves have dried, remove them, dust the tuber with a fungicide such as captan and bury it in dry peat moss. The temperature of the storage should be 5° to 7°C. Most basements are too warm and over the winter the bulb will simply dehydrate in the higher temperatures of 20° to 21°C. You really need a place like a root cellar to store the bulb.

Should I do nothing with it all winter?

Right. Then bring it out sometime in March and plant it up near the surface of very peaty soil, in a pot, moistening the peat. It should start up again in two to three weeks and you've got the plant for another year.

Tuberous Begonias are photoperiodic — they respond to ever-shortening fall days by beginning to go dormant and putting energy into the tuber rather than the leaves. Many Tuberous Begonias that are available in the spring in garden centres are grown from seed and they will not develop a tuber of any size under our normal fall conditions — they freeze before the day length is really short enough to trigger the plant into partial dormancy and tuber production. So if you want to increase the size of the tuber or begin the tuber from a seed-produced Tuberous Begonia, then you must continue them growing later into the fall. To prevent termination of growth due to temperatures below 10°C, garden-grown plants should be potted into 20 cm pots and moved to a bright sunny window indoors. Tuberous Begonias grown in pots on a patio or balcony should be treated the same way so that the tuber will continue to grow. Larger tubers mean larger flowers the following year. Spraying with benomyl or captan will help prevent destructive fungus disease on the foliage.

During this period of time the plant must be subjected only to normal day length. Artificial light that extends the duration of a normal fall day may prevent the growth of the tuber. Give the plant full sun during the day and total darkness in a cupboard or under an opaque covering at night. If the plant is in a window you may be able to accomplish this by simply pulling the drapes when you turn on the lights in the evening.

In late October let them dry out and put them into storage as described earlier. You can get them to flower earlier the following spring by putting the tubers under eighteen to twenty-four hours of artificial light in a lighting unit beginning in February. You should have plants in bloom and bud by May.

If you want to start new Tuberous Begonias from seed you should sow in January. You will also have to extend the day length to at least sixteen to eighteen hours by artificial light in order to prevent the small seedling, as it germinates, from responding to the short winter day length, going dormant and never growing properly. In fact, lighting them twenty-four hours a day encourages maximum growth rate. This must be continued right up into late March when the days are naturally long enough to promote growth and flowering.

Oleanders

I have an Oleander and I want to know the best way to keep it over the winter.

Oleander is a tropical or subtropical plant and if it receives severe frost it is going to be killed. I know people who winter over these plants in small plastic lean-tos on the side of their houses facing south, with a connection to an open cellar window. In this way they get enough heat to prevent severe frost. You can often keep even Citrus trees over in this manner.

Can I keep it in the house?

Yes, it is quite possible to winter over an Oleander in the house. It does require a lot of light, which means placing it directly in an east, west or south window.

Do I prune it in the winter?

No. The best time to prune is in the bright-light period of spring or summer to encourage the plant to form new branches and buds, and prevent it from wandering out of its space. I do not believe that you will be able to get it to flower during the low-light period of the winter when it is in the home but as the light increases in the spring or when you put it out in a shady spot in the garden in the summer, it should flower very well.

How much watering should I do in the winter?

It will probably work out to be once every couple of weeks, but really the only adequate test is to feel the soil. When that is dry, water it thoroughly. I would do no feeding during the dull winter months and leach it just prior to the high-light period of the spring.

The natural growth of many Oleanders is very sparse and disjointed, making a rather unattractive shrub in the initial stages. It never ceases to amaze me how the most gawky-shaped shrub will be bought and taken home as a desirable-looking plant. It might be because people have seen Oleanders growing in the tropics during one of their vacations and want to transfer that nostalgia to their home. Pruning and summer vacations in a shady spot in the garden can, however, produce a rather attractive indoor foliage plant during the winter or an outdoor flowering shrub or tree during the summer. In the spring there are now available new dwarf, self-branching Oleanders which are more ornamental shrubs and trees for balcony or patio containers.

Tropical Evergreen Makes a Suitable Christmas Tree

I have heard that you can use a potted native evergreen as a Christmas tree. Will it survive this treatment?

I would not recommend it. The risk of losing the tree is very high. It has to be nursery grown and potted before frost. Then it must be stored by the nursery in temperature-controlled, plastic-covered greenhouses until Christmas. These structures provide just enough light to prevent deterioration while the trees remain dormant. Even a few days in the high home temperatures and the presence of even higher localized temperatures caused by decorative lights could initiate hormone changes that start new growth. The soil ball will most certainly thaw out completely and when the evergreen is returned to winter temperatures that could be -15° to -20°C, the tree would not likely survive.

Do you have a better suggestion for a live Christmas tree?

Yes, I do. The tropical evergreen commonly called the Norfolk Island Pine does the job beautifully.

Are they expensive?

Foot for foot, they cost no more than a plastic tree and they surely are more satisfying to look at all year round.

Being a tropical tree, it would have to be kept on as a house plant. How would I care for it?

With the overcast skies that come our way in winter in these latitudes and the low-light intensity of the sun whenever it does peek through, the main requirement of your plant is to be placed as close as possible to an east, south or west window.

What about watering?

The plant needs uniform moisture with minor dryings out between waterings to let air into the soil. While they will tolerate a fairly severe drying out, it may stunt the growth of some of the branch tips and affect the symmetry of the plant. With the resumption of normal watering, the subsequent branches will be longer than the stunted growth. The Norfolk Island Pine is also subject to root rot if the soil is kept saturated with water for any length of time. The needles, particularly the older ones, will yellow, turn brown and drop. A monthly check of the root ball (see page 20) is essential until a proper watering routine is established.

What about summer care when the light intensity is higher?

As with other plants, during high-light periods it can be moved back from the window. It can also be put out on a patio or in a garden in a shaded spot so that it continues to grow under relatively low light. Then it will adjust back into the indoor winter light with less needle drop.

Not a true pine, the correct botanical name is Araucaria heterophylla. Other conifers that also make hardy house plants are the Monkey Puzzle Tree or Araucaria bidwillii and members of the genus Podocarpus, commonly called Buddhist Pine or Southern Yew. While Norfolk Pine will tolerate very low light levels (as low as fifteen foot candles) for a week or two (should you want it in a darker place for Christmas), it should be kept close to a good light source for the balance of the winter months. They will thrive close to an unobstructed north window if bought as a small plant (up to 20 cm), but larger plants seldom acclimatize to northern light.

In commercial horticulture Norfolk Island Pine are propagated from seed, but during the winter months you may propagate by air layering a cutting from the top of the plant, should your specimen become too tall (see Chapter 8). However, any pruning of the plant will permanently stop the growth of that point pruned. Unlike many other conifers it is impossible to brace up a side branch and get the Norfolk Island Pine to resume upright growth once the primary growing tip is removed. Even when directed skyward, a horizontal branch always has the characteristic of a side branch. So jealously guard that growing tip if you want the tree to continue upwards and have the symmetrical, whorled growth which is so attractive. Once it is removed, the tree only grows horizontally.

Norfolk Island Pine grow best at normal room temperatures, but they will tolerate dips down to the freezing mark. Low temperatures, however, turn the plant brown. This chill does not cause permanent damage providing they do not receive severe frost. As soon as the temperature climbs again the plant will regain its characteristic lush green colour.

Chapter 8
Propagation

Rooting Cuttings

I would like to take cuttings of my outdoor Geranium and Impatiens plants over the winter so that I will have a supply of new plants for replanting in the garden next spring. How do I do this?

Taking cuttings from Geraniums and Impatiens is a good way to perpetuate these plants from year to year. Just make sure that these plants do not receive any frost before taking cuttings in the fall — Geraniums that receive even light frost may not show visible damage but will not root. A month before taking cuttings you should clean off all dead blooms from the plants that you are going to use as parent plants and spray them with benomyl fungicide, repeating this about two weeks later. This will help eliminate stem rot caused by latent Botrytis fungus spores which incubate under the moist conditions of propagation.

Mature Impatiens plants with heavy, well-developed branches in flower almost invariably produce "palm tree" cuttings that will never branch out. To avoid this, cut back the parent plant by half of its growth if it has been growing unchecked for more than six weeks. When the new growth has developed two mature leaves, leaving two new leaves on the same branch of the parent, take this short cutting. Smaller cuttings from side growth are less likely to be terminally or apically dominant (non-branching) than top cuttings.

Preparing and Taking Cuttings

Any propagation method involving severing a portion of a plant from the parent is major surgery. As in all surgery, the success of the operation depends to a great degree on the health of the "patient" involved. Most house plants propagate more readily when they are in active growth, i.e. during the high-light times of the year. If artificial light is the energy source, propagation can be done at any time of the year, provided the light is sufficient to promote vigorous, compact growth. New growth produced at borderline light levels is often soft (as anyone who has ever attempted to propagate Geraniums or Impatiens in January or February can confirm). Large, light green, soft leaves that wilt readily when the sun pops out after a long dark spell are a sign of soft growth that will be difficult to propagate. Stems that are weak and stretchy, with leaves spaced far apart, are equally difficult to root. A plant that is just maintaining itself is having enough difficulty surviving without attempting to propagate it. A parent plant that has suffered root injury by overfertilizing or overwatering will also make propagation very risky.

Additional light will help correct this, as well allowing minor wilting between thorough waterings. This hardens the wood of the stem and the tissue of the leaves. If soft new growth is not conditioned by adequate light and periods of minor wilting, it is often impossible to avoid the subsequent rotting of the cutting. However, at the actual time of taking cuttings, the parent plant should be full of water with no wilting evident.

In the summer and early fall this is seldom a problem. Indeed, sunlight, air movement, and increased transpiration at high-light seasons may result in excessive drying out of the soil. This can produce very hard wood that is equally reluctant to root. In this case the cutting will root faster if it is short and close to the growing tip.

The length of the cutting can vary, but it should include the growing tip with between two to four mature leaves. Beyond where the last mature leaf joins the stem, you need a further stem length of approximately 2 cm to anchor the plant in the rooting media. This is particularly important on plants that grow generally upright, such as Geraniums or Impatiens. An upright-growing plant that has been rooted with no stem below grade will eventually topple. The rooting speed is the same at any point on the stem. The bottom of the cutting does not have to be at a leaf node where the leaf joins the stem.

The best method of taking the cutting is to snap it off in the same way that you would check the freshness of a green bean. If the stem will not snap clean, leaving no bruise, then you should use a sharp knife. Bruised tissue does not generate new cells and provides an entry point for disease. A knife, however, unless sterilized between taking cuttings from each different parent plant, can transmit disease. One part household bleach to ten parts water is a satisfactory sterilant for both knives and used containers. Used clay pots should also be scrubbed with a brush to remove saline deposits.

It is not essential that a leaf be removed if a portion of the leaf petiole ends up below the soil. Leaves store plant food that the cutting will need. Also, any leaf removal makes an open wound on the stem and increases the possibility of a disease organism attacking the cutting at this point. However, any leaf or leaf axil sheath which is below grade must be removed. If they are buried in the media, they will die, rot and often cause disease problems. The axil sheath can generally be removed by pulling sharply towards the bottom of the cutting. A healthy cutting will heal right at the main stem.

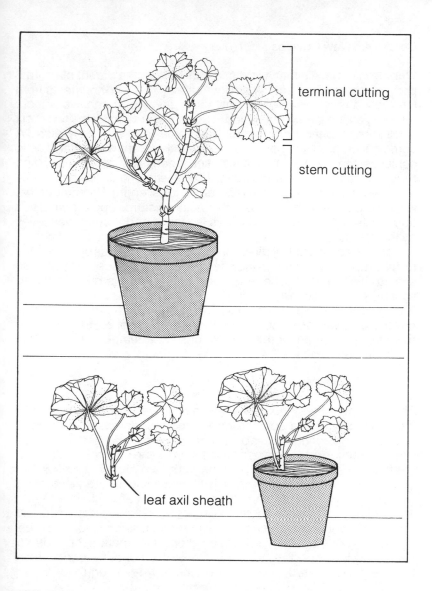

terminal cutting

stem cutting

leaf axil sheath

TOP. *Both terminal and stem cuttings can be propagated from the same Geranium plant, although terminal cuttings root more quickly. More than one stem cutting consisting of two mature leaves may be taken from the same stem until the hard woody stem is reached. Any stem cutting should be cut off just above the uppermost leaf as this portion of the stem cutting will die off anyway. New branches will appear where the leaf petiole joins the stem.*

BOTTOM. *If necessary, remove the bottom leaf or two to clear 2 to 3 cm of the stem which will be inserted in soil. Also remove the leaf axil sheath.*

93

Care of the New Cuttings

When you remove either a leaf or a cutting from the parent plant, that portion has no roots and its ability to absorb water or nutrients from the rooting media is minimal until roots develop. It can live without nutrients on the stored plant food in the leaf and stem for the two to six week rooting period provided it has come from a healthy plant. A combination of misting and surrounding the plant with clear plastic achieves the high humidity situation necessary for rooting, and reduces water stress from drafts. The plastic should be held away from the cutting a distance at least equal to its length. Remember that while the plant is in this process the main moisture supply is what you apply externally to the leaves. This is maintained around the leaves by the plastic.

Light is necessary, but direct sunlight does put stress on the leaves to take up more water to satisfy growth processes. Propagation should therefore be done in a place where there is bright diffused light but no direct sunlight.

Another factor that influences rooting is temperature. While many house plants will root at normal room temperature of 20° to 21°C, most of them will have an increased response at a temperature of 26° to 28°C (see page 114).

Rooting Hormones

The use of rooting hormone (usually a very dilute strength of indulbutyric acid in a powder form) generally increases the amount and speed of rooting. Available in three different strengths, the basic rule of selection is that the harder the stem of the cutting, the stronger the hormone chosen. However, only your own experimentation with and without hormone can establish its benefits to the plants you want to propagate. On soft cuttings of some plants it can injure plant tissue and delay or preclude rooting. Cuttings from most house plants would only benefit from the weakest hormone formulation (Number 1). The end of the cutting should be dipped to about a 2 cm depth, then sharply rapped against the rim of the hormone container to remove any excess. Just a thin film of the powder is required.

Rooting Media

It is possible to root cuttings by immersing the bottom of the stem in fresh water. This procedure minimizes the initial shock because the cutting can take up water more readily, though having developed roots in water, it has to adjust later when you put it in soil. The water method usually results in a longer nursing period than rooting directly in a proper rooting media. The best method is to root in a very porous rooting media which may or may not contain any soil. It should be pasteurized, free of disease and porous so that there is plenty of air present around that stem to help generate a root system (the peat-lite mix discussed in Chapter 1 is ideal). Choose 6 to 10 cm pots set firmly on the same rooting media in a tray at least 8 cm deep. In this way you will achieve an increase in drainage capability as discussed on page 18. If you are not rooting enough cuttings at one time to warrant the use of the tray, then simply stack the pots two deep, both filled with the same rooting media.

If you have had problems with cuttings rotting, even in a sterilized rooting media, drench the soil with a combination of the fungicides captan and benomyl diluted in water before inserting the cutting. In cases of persistent rot problems, this same mixture can be again drenched onto both cuttings and media two weeks later. The fungicide will also help control any latent fungus spores on the cutting.

Cuttings can simply be pushed into a soft, moist media to proper depth or into preformed holes if the stems are brittle. Firm the media only sufficiently to hold the cutting in position. Do not pack or flood the media after sticking in the cutting. This will drive out necessary air and promote waterlogging. Once new roots are evident, then water thoroughly.

Maintenance of Cuttings

Misting cuttings to supply water that would normally come from the root system must be done frequently enough to prevent major wilting. Major wilting will delay rooting and may be serious enough to cause cell damage, leaf loss, and death. Minor limpness in the leaves, for a few days after the cutting has been taken, is normal, but a ragging down of the foliage in a full wilt must be corrected immediately by more frequent misting. The best misting tool is the popular 500 ml plastic canister with a finger-operated trigger pump. If you keep it 30 cm away from the cuttings the mist will be at prevailing air temperature as it settles on the cuttings. Water should be applied each time until a film of moisture begins to run off the leaves.

The leaves of some plants have such substance that, in the rooting process, they can be dying and even dead without actually manifesting the symptoms of wilting. Feel a leaf on the parent plant in a state of turgor after watering and compare this with the leaves of the cutting to determine whether or not misting frequency is sufficient.

Misting a cutting during the rooting process is something like watering a plant: there is no mathematical formula that can be followed. Mist as frequently as is necessary to prevent major wilting until roots appear.

Rooting Speed

If you have begun with a cutting or plant part from a healthy plant and have controlled the environmental factors, then rooting should take place within ten days to three weeks and be fully accomplished by three to six weeks. Rooting can be determined by gently tugging on the plant. When roots have begun the plant will resist this tugging. At this point the plant begins to be able to take up some of its own water and the weaning process (the reduction of the frequency of misting and removing the plastic covering) can begin. If the incubator environment is carried too long beyond the appearance of the roots, then growth will be very soft and will not adjust easily to the real world.

When the initial roots appear, begin to space out the interval of any misting. A day or two later, remove the plastic covering for a period each day until minor wilting is observed. Then mist the cuttings lightly and cover with the plastic bag. Leave it on only long enough for the plant to become turgid again. Then repeat the process. Before many days it should be necessary only to mist without applying the plastic bag. The acclimatizing process should be complete in a week to ten days and the plant should then thrive in the normal household environment.

Fertilizing

If you are using peat-lite mix, which is very low in nutrients, then fertilizing can be done with a 20-20-20 water-soluble fertilizer with trace elements as soon as root initials appear. This can also be combined with a fungicide if necessary. Repeat the fertilizer with every watering for the first six to eight weeks of the cutting's growth. By then it will be necessary to transplant the cuttings into a larger pot. Do not disturb the new root system. Simply add soil around it, keeping the plant at the same depth. Cease all fertilizing until the weather begins to get bright in the spring, unless there is rapid, continuous growth.

The plant can be returned to its normal light situation as soon as the weaning process is complete. Should it still not receive enough light to cause it to branch out then I would suggest that you take the tip of the plant just as if you were taking another cutting; either root that tip or throw it away. This pinching process causes the plant to branch out and keeps it more compact.

Root Division

I have two Baby's Tears plants that are lovely and green on top but they are dying underneath. What can I do about this?

How long have they been growing?

About a year.

Is the part that is green a thick mat-like growth on the surface?

Yes, but the brown part is beginning to work its way up towards the surface.

Over the period of a year the plant has reached maturity and those older leaves are bound to age, turn brown and fall off. This process is accelerated as the new leaves cut off the light from the older leaves. In order to let light in for the older growth it is often necessary to take a pair of scissors with a very fine point and thin out the growth. Cut off some of the stems at or just above the pot line and take the whole stem out. This thins out the growth and allows more light to penetrate, keeping the older leaves active longer. There will come a point, however, when this method will no longer rejuvenate the plant and you will simply have to cut it back, subdivide and replant it.

The best method of propagating Baby's Tears is to cut back the older plants but not beyond the point where there are green leaves. If you cut back into the dead leaves, you will have no leaf area to support the plant during propagation. Knock the older plant out of its pot, and rather ruthlessly start to pull apart a small section of the root system together with the upper part of the plant. In this way you will end up with small tufts of stems, leaves and roots.

The cutting back of the leaves is necessary because the separation of the roots will drastically reduce the amount of roots and hence the number of leaves that can be supported. This subdivision of the plant will injure the root system and it will be necessary to mist the young divisions and cover them with clear plastic. Place them in bright diffused light but not in direct sunlight. Within a few days you should be able to wean them away from this special treatment by removing the plastic and letting them slowly go back to normal conditions as they begin to put on new growth. The little tufts can be transplanted into single 6 cm pots. Over a period of a few weeks in diffused light they will soon cover the surface of the pots. You may use a larger pot of any diameter, using a good open potting soil, and transplant several tufts, spacing them about 5 cm apart. Again, they will soon cover the surface and begin to trail down.

Side Shoots

My Bromeliad is having little babies, off-shoots around the base of the plant. Can I plant them separately and induce them to flower again?

Bromeliad is a family name covering a broad group of air root (epiphytic) plants. The tropical pineapple comes from a plant in that family. One common ornamental of the family is the Aechmea fasciata. It has a shell-burst of wide green thick foliage with an overcast gray, almost scale-like appearance and black spiny edges. The foliage forms a vase in the centre that actually holds water and out of this vase comes a long stem with a burst of bloom on the top that looks like the still photo of a fireworks display. It is mostly pinkish in colour but the actual flower is blue, round and spread throughout this pinkish bract.

Yes, that's the one. The flower has lasted for weeks and weeks and lately I just noticed these tiny plantlets coming from around the bottom. It would be great fun to produce another plant like this one.

Fun it is. When the offshoots are about one quarter the size of the parent plant they should have developed a root system of their own below the soil. At that point take a sharp knife and perform Siamese Twin surgery on the plants. Cut them off and away from the parent, taking as much of the root system as possible. The parent plant will not reflower and is usually discarded during the operation. Divide the root system evenly between the offshoots in the same manner as you would cut up a pie. Less root damage will be done this way than if you try to pull apart the root system attached to each offshoot.

In the tropics Bromeliads grow in the trees on decaying plant matter, so they need a moist, porous rooting and growing soil. Plant them in the same-sized pot as your parent plant was in and at the same depth that it was when it was attached to the parent.

How long will it take to grow to the size of the existing one?

They are normally mature in about three years but it depends on how much light they receive and the humidity in your home. In the winter they would benefit from direct sunlight from November through February. During the rest of the year bright diffused light will be fine. Because of their jungle origin they love lots of humidity so a mechanical humidifier on your furnace plus grouping them with other plants will also benefit.

Should I keep the vase formed by the leaves full of water?

Yes. They draw much of their moisture and nutrients from this supply. If it becomes green with algae just dump it out, gently wash out the vase and refill it with a half strength solution of water-soluble 20-20-20 fertilizer. Fertilize the root system as well during the summer months.

Will it then flower?

Yes. Under good conditions in about three years. In their native habitat the supplicant formation of the leaves collects rain and falling organic matter from trees. In the presence of warm tropical temperatures and water the decaying leaves give off minute quantities of ethylene gas. At the time of maturity the gas initiates budset and subsequent flower development. You can duplicate these conditions by growing the plant actively until it is about the size of your present plant. Place the plant in a clear plastic bag along with cut up pieces of fruit such as an apple and close the bag. As it decomposes the apple will give off ethylene gas. One to two weeks of this treatment should be sufficient to initiate the bud. Avoid direct sunlight during the plastic bag treatment, as this would cause excessive temperatures inside the bag. It may take up to six months before the flower is fully mature depending on the genus and the amount of light available.

Isn't that fascinating. I am going to try it.

Ethylene gas, while not harmful to humans in minute quantities, is the deadly enemy of much plant material. A Carnation in the presence of as little ethylene gas as 0.2 parts per million will fold up and die in a matter of hours. In the presence of 4 to 6 parts per million of ethylene gas a growing plant of the Easter Lily will curl up as if it had been sprayed with weed killer (an entire crop was destroyed in one greenhouse by the presence of a welder cutting metal with acetylene gas in a building attached to the greenhouse). Yet many members of the Bromeliad family respond positively to the presence of ethylene gas, and indeed it is necessary for the formation of buds. If you want quicker results than the cut-up apple and plastic bag method, take your Bromeliad to your local welding shop. Bubble a short burst of acetylene gas from an ordinary welder's torch into the water in the vase. Gas from a domestic butane blow torch will also work.

Air Layering

I have a Cut-leaf Philodendron and one stem is growing way up above the bark on which the rest of the plant is tied. Can I root a cutting off the top of it?

If you want to propagate the plant, I would suggest that you air layer the cutting rather than cutting it right off. Air layering means putting roots on the stem of the plant while part of the stem is still attached to the parent plant. This method requires a lot less care on your part because the cutting, while it is rooting, is still attached to the parent and can get its water supply from this source. With the Cut-leaf Philodendron the stem is thick enough to do this quite readily. You can also tame your Philodendron without taking a cutting off it. Take a pair of pliers that will open up sufficiently to go over the thick stem of the plant. Cover the jaws of the pliers with bandaids so that the teeth do not crush the stem too severely. Take the pliers and ruthlessly crush about a 10 cm section of the stem just above the top of the bark. Now take the upper part of the stem, bend it over and tie it close to the existing stake. Within a few days the leaves and growing tip will turn around and look up as they should. This will give your plant a bushy, attractive appearance, covering any of the old part of the plant that has become unsightly. There is no reason why you couldn't put a double loop in the stem if you need to make it fit the stake that it is growing on. If there are brown air roots in your way, simply cut them off.

To root by air layering, choose a portion of the stem that is still relatively green. The harder the stem and the more brown bark that has developed, the slower the rooting and the greater the risk of failure. The cutting being propagated may be up to 75 cm long.

It may be necessary to remove leaves from 10 to 15 cm of the stem to make a clear space for the air layering process. Some species of plants will "bleed" latex sap but don't be concerned about this. It will soon stop.

Take a very sharp knife and cut diagonally half way through the stem as indicated. When the latex stops apply Number 1 rooting hormone to the upper edge of the cut with a Q-tip.

Open up the cut by bending the stem slightly, and stuff into the cut a small quantity of coarse sphagnum moss, using the dull edge of the knife. This is to prevent the stem from healing back together, aborting the rooting process.

Thoroughly soak a double handful of sphagnum moss for half an hour or more in lukewarm water. (Working with sphagnum moss is a great cleanser and softener of chapped hands, incidentally.) Remove the sphagnum from the water and squeeze out all excess

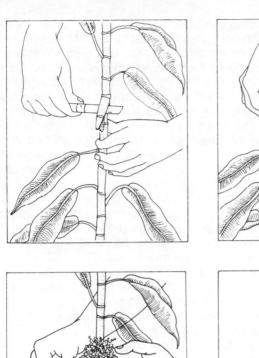
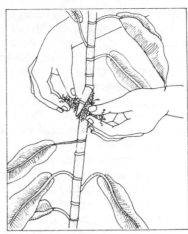
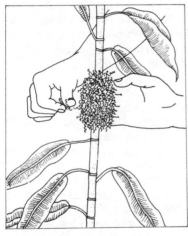
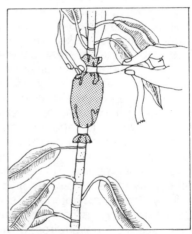

TOP LEFT. *Remove enough leaves to clear 10 to 15 cm of the stem. With a sharp knife, make an upward incision at approximately a 45 degree angle half-way through the stem at the centre of the cleared portion.*

TOP RIGHT. *Carefully bending the stem to open the incision and using your fingers or the dull edge of the knife, push enough moist sphagnum moss into the incision to prevent the sides of the incision from touching.*

BOTTOM LEFT. *Place a handful of thoroughly moistened sphagnum moss around the incision.*

BOTTOM RIGHT. *Holding the sphagnum in place with one hand, wrap a plastic sheet around the moss and tie the top and bottom.*

water. Apply the double handful around the cut.

Wrap the sphagnum with one or two layers of plastic from a cleaner's bag or food wrap to keep the moss in place and retain moisture. Tie it at the top and bottom. Cover the moss with aluminum foil or use a black plastic sheet to keep out the light, to prevent algae from growing. There should be sufficient moisture present from the initial wet moss to last through the rooting process, but check carefully after two weeks and moisten the moss if necessary. Depending on the hardness of the stem and the health of the plant, roots will become visible after four to six weeks. When there is a well-developed root system, remove the plastic. With minimum disturbance to the moss, locate the uncut portion of the stem, nick it deeply opposite the original cut, and gently bend the stem away from the original cut until it snaps off. Some plants will snap off readily without cutting. Leaving the moss intact, plant the rooted cutting into a 15 to 20 cm pot in potting soil at a depth that completely covers the moss and anchors the plant. Firm the soil gently and water thoroughly.

If the parent plant is hard, woody and has developed bark, mist it thoroughly and wrap loosely or cover the whole plant loosely with a clear plastic cleaner's bag. A single branch from which a cutting has been rooted may be treated the same way. Remove the bag and mist again if condensation disappears off the inside of the bag. The warmth and high humidity will help "sweat out" new branches from the old woody stem. Do not overwater the parent plant at this point if you have removed all or most of the leaf area. With no leaves to transpire water, its requirements are minimal. The plastic should be removed as soon as new growth tips are plainly visible.

The best time of the year to propagate is probably during the spring and summer months. This is a high-light period. The cutting will root and grow more vigorously and the parent plant will branch more readily. The more light the parent plant receives after the cutting has been removed, the more branches will be initiated. Placing the parent plant in direct sunlight from a window is fine, provided the temperature under the plastic does not rise above 30°C. If in doubt about the temperature, hang a thermometer inside the plastic wrap.

CAUTION: Do not move the plant while it is in the rooting process. Any sudden movement may snap off the cutting before it is rooted. If you must move it, brace it well with a long splint reaching well above and below the rooting area of the stem.

Soil Layering

Could you tell me what I could do to revive my very straggly-looking Philodendron plant? It is difficult to know what to do with it to improve the appearance.

This is the vine-type Philodendron with heart shaped leaves?

Yes, it is.

Try this. Repot the Philodendron into a pot at least two sizes larger than the present pot using a potting soil containing at least two-thirds peat moss. Trim off any yellow or defective leaves. Scarify the root system lightly and place it in the new pot at the same depth as it was originally. Fill around with clean potting soil. Now take the vine and carefully coil it round and round near the rim of the new pot so that most of the vine touches the soil. It may go around two or three times or more. Don't be concerned about removing the odd leaf that won't come into place. Press the vine firmly down onto the potting soil and pin it into position

Any vine-type plant can be refurbished by repotting it into a larger pot and coiling the vine or vines around the pot on the surface of the soil. Hairpins or partially straightened paper clips can be used to hold the vine firmly on the surface of the soil. Remove any leaves that prevent the vine from making contact with the soil. Pinch out the tip to encourage branching.

using a hairpin that has been spread slightly so that it goes over the stem without bruising it or a paper clip that has been opened into a U-shape. Pinch out 5 cm of the growing tip of the Philodendron. If there is a spot of open soil left in this repotting operation then stick that growing tip into the potting soil to root. Mist it frequently, cover it with clear plastic and put it in bright diffused light. The misting will soften the tissue of the plant and cause it to branch out. Mist for two to three weeks until you see new branches coming where the leaf petiole joins the vine of the plant. Before long you should have a lush green-looking Philodendron that will begin to vine down again. This soil layering rehabilitation technique will work on almost any viny green plant: Ivy, Pothos, Nephthytis, Dipladenia, Hoya. The plant will root wherever the trailing stem touches the soil firmly. This method will also work as a propagating technique on plants such as Chlorophytum (Spider Plant) or Cissus rhombifolia (Grape Ivy).

A hairpin or partially straightened paper clip can be used to press the leader of a Spider Plant runner firmly onto the moistened surface of the rooting media as close as possible to the plantlet. Because the plantlet remains attached to the parent, no misting or plastic cover is needed, nor does the light have to be reduced. If this method is physically awkward because of the location of the parent plant then cut off the plantlet and root it in the same manner as a cutting. Rooting is accomplished in a couple of weeks with either method.

Cissus rhombifolia can be difficult to root as a terminal cutting. Pin about 5 cm of an actively growing stem down onto the moistened surface of a pot filled with potting soil. A longer branch may also be coiled around the surface of a 10 or 15 cm pot, pinned in several places and cut from the parent plant when roots form in two to four weeks. No misting or plastic is required with this method.

OPPOSITE. *Plants like the Chlorophytum (Spider Plant) can be readily propagated by pressing the plantlet down into the surface of porous potting soil until it has rooted.*

Leaf Propagation

I was given some Begonia cuttings. They are the longest cuttings I have ever seen. Most of them are about 30 cm long and leaves are about 15 cm across and 8 cm long. The friend who had grown them had taken them off the parent plant and put them in water for the longest time but nothing ever happened. Is there a different method of rooting Begonias?

I believe that you are describing the Rex Begonia. Is the leaf long, serrated and pointed?

Exactly.

There is an entirely different method of propagating Rex Begonias. Simply cut the leaf from the parent plant. Select a very open potting soil that drains readily. A mixture of two-thirds peat moss and one-third vermiculite or perlite will work very well. Put the soil in a pot of a diameter slightly larger than the leaf. Lay the leaf down on the surface of the soil and take a very sharp knife. Put incisions in the largest veins of the leaf—the ones that come out from the centre stem like the fingers of a hand. Cut these veins right through. The leaf between the veins should be left intact. Then pin the leaf down with a hairpin or partially straightened paper clip so that the incisions are firmly pressed against the surface of the soil.

The techniques of misting, use of clear plastic and temperature as discussed regarding cuttings also apply here. You will notice in three to six weeks that little plants will begin right where you have made the cuts in the leaf, and roots will go down into the soil. As soon as the new plants have established a couple of true leaves they can be separated from the mother leaf. By this time there will be roots so that you can transplant them into an open soil similar to the one you have already used.

With Tolmiea menziesii (Piggyback Plant) the leaf propagating technique is slightly different from Rex Begonia. In this case the plantlet, under sufficient light, will already be evident as it grows on the parent plant. Often these parent leaves are far too large to fit on the surface of a 6 cm pot and they can be trimmed with scissors. Then the leaf can be pinned to the moistened surface of the rooting media. Roots should be evident in three to five weeks. At this time, the rest of the old leaf should be cut away and discarded.

Another variation of leaf propagation is Sedum morganianum (Burro's Tails). The leaves can be removed and pressed firmly into the surface of the rooting media in a horizontal position. The short leaf stem should rest on the surface of the moist media. Both plantlets and roots will emerge from this point. Several leaves can be placed on the surface of a hanging container about 3 cm apart. They can be allowed to grow to maturity without transplanting, making a full, attractive hanging plant.

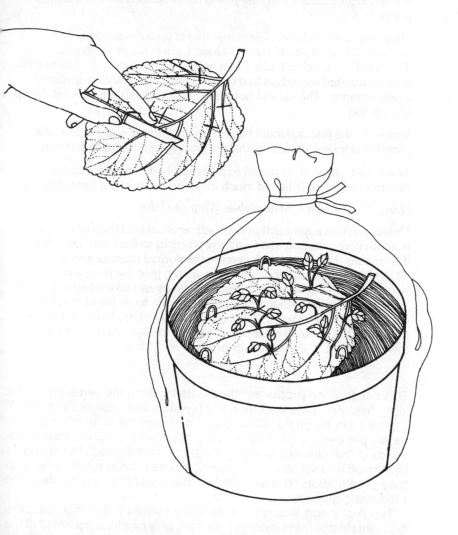

Rex Begonia is best propagated by cutting off a healthy leaf that has recently reached maturity. Cut right through the larger veins, leaving the body of the leaf intact. Pin the leaf down onto the surface of porous potting soil with hairpins or partially straightened paper clips so that the incisions touch the surface of the rooting media. Plantlets will appear at the incisions, sending roots down into the rooting media.

Viviparous Leaf Propagation

I have a plant that appears to be in trouble but I don't know the name of it. It has jagged leaves and little plants are produced on these jagged points.

There are two species of Kalanchoe that fit your description. The common name of one of them is Good Luck Plant or Mother of Thousands. The other is Life Plant or Mother of Hundreds. The first has sharply serrated leaf edges that normally produce plantlets at almost every serration. The second normally only produces a plantlet at the tip of each leaf.

It must be the first one that I have. The only problem is that the little plantlets stopped appearing and the growth has slowed way down.

This is mid winter and I would expect this plant to respond in this manner to the low light and much lower humidity in our heated homes.

I have it in the best light available. What can I do?

Unless you can augment that light with artificial light then all you can do is adjust your watering and fertilizing practices to the lower growth rate. This means that you should water in the normal manner and withhold all fertilizing. At least once during the winter, give the plant a good two-hour leaching which will wash the leaves and take away any excess salts (see page 29). Anything that you can do to increase the humidity, either with a humidifier or by grouping it with other plants, would help. I am sure that as the humidity goes up and the light intensity increases towards spring, it will resume its productive lifestyle.

This plant, which produces little plants all along the serrations of the leaf, has the botanical name of Kalanchoe daigremontiana X tubiflora. Under bright diffused light and high humidity in the sixty to eighty per cent range, this amazing plant will produce literally thousands of little plantlets all along the edges of every leaf. These can be broken off and set on a good rooting media to propagate. Otherwise they usually drop off when still tiny and multiply wherever they find favourable ground.

The fleshy egg-shaped leaves of the related Kalanchoe gastonis bonnieri (Mother of Hundreds) normally only produce a plantlet at the tip, which will even produce roots while on the parent if the humidity is high enough. If the leaf touches down on soil it will also produce plantlets along the rest of the edge of the leaf. The plant produces a tall flower cluster in pale pink. Because of their unique multiplication capacity they make real conversation pieces as houseplants. In plant multiplication this process is called viviparous propagation. Think how intrigued your friends will be if you let it be known you are involved in viviparous propagation.

Plantlets that form on some species of Kalanchoe can readily be propagated by cutting them off the parent or by touching the parent leaf and plantlet down onto the surface of a rooting media. Cutting away from the parent can then be done in two or three weeks.

With some succulents such as the Crassula (Jade Plant) there is a modification of the leaf cutting technique that induces viviparous plantlets. Using a healthy Jade leaf, leaving it attached to parent, cut part way through the leaf across the top and bend the leaf back exposing the cut surface but still leaving the bottom of the leaf attached. Leave it four days to a week to callous over and then snap the cut portion off and insert it no more than 1 cm into rooting media. Observe all the foregoing techniques of propagating leaf parts. In three to six weeks several plantlets and root systems should appear emanating from the submerged cut edge. When the new leaves are 0.5 cm in diameter, cut each plantlet away and discard the parent leaf. Plantlets can be planted and nurtured carefully in bright light with misting until established.

The thick fleshy leaf of the Jade Plant allows you to cut part way through the leaf and fold the tip down to open up the incision. Four days to a week later, the incision will have calloused. The leaf tip can then be removed and stuck 1 cm deep into rooting media. Roots and plantlets will originate from the calloused edge.

Leaf Petiole Propagation

How do I propagate my African Violets?

Saintpaulia (African Violet) can be propagated from leaf petioles. Cut the leaf blade and petiole from the parent plant, leaving the petiole 2 to 5 cm long. Insert the leaf stem to a depth of 2 cm into a moist rooting media (peat-lite mix would be ideal). In four to eight weeks roots and shoots will develop from the end of the petiole. Plantlets may rise from the end of the petiole below the soil or from the central rib of the leaf blade if this is touching the rooting media.

When the emerging leaves forming a cluster are about 1 cm in diameter, the plantlets should be gently lifted from the media. Cut them apart with a sharp knife into individual plants and plant them separately into 6 cm pots at the same depth at which they rooted. Most of the growing media will fall away from the root system in this operation and misting may be required until new roots are formed.

The Rieger Begonia (Schwabenland type) can also be propagated this way, although these plants are thermo and photoperiodic, which means that they flower, root and branch out with the correct manipulation of temperature and day length. To propagate the single-flowered upright type (the double-flowered, pendulous Aphrodite type is best taken as a terminal cutting), select a healthy leaf about 8 cm in diameter and cut the petiole at a point about 2 cm down from the leaf. The roots and shoots are developed from the base of the petiole. It usually forms roots within two weeks but it takes three and a half months to develop the shoots and ready the plantlets for potting.

The best temperature for the rooting and branching out of the new plantlets is 18°C. If the parent plant from which the leaf cuttings are taken can be placed in temperatures of 15°C and given a short-day treatment of thirteen hours' darkness and eleven hours' full light for three weeks before propagating any leaves (mid-April and mid-September are good times for this), the number of branches from the base of the petiole will be greatly increased.

When the plantlets are about 5 cm high the old leaf may be removed. When the largest leaves are 3 to 5 cm in diameter, lift the plantlets out of the rooting media and cut them apart into individual plants before transplanting. Again they will grow best at a temperature of about 18°C. Temperatures of 21° and 22°C tend to cause them to stretch. As long as they receive more than thirteen hours of light, either by natural or artificial source, they will seldom bloom. To initiate flowering, the day length should be shortened to about ten hours of bright light or bright fluorescent light and fourteen hours of darkness for a period of about three weeks. This is usually enough to induce flowering. After this they will go on flowering regardless of day length for a long period of time.

Riegers do not respond well to misting. Necessary moisture is best maintained around the propagating leaf by covering it with clear or white plastic. The initial moistening of the rooting media prior to sticking in the leaf should supply the required moisture if plastic is used.

TOP. *A healthy leaf is cut from the parent and the leaf petiole is pushed 2 cm deep in moist rooting media, misted and covered with clear plastic. In four to eight weeks roots grow down into the media and shoots emerge from the buried end of the petiole.*

BOTTOM. *When the emerging leaves are about 1 cm in diameter they are dug up, cut apart into individual plantlets and planted separately into about 6 cm pots. The parent leaf is discarded.*

Seed Germination

I have just found an old paper package of flower seeds that has been sitting in my basement for over a year. Will they germinate if I plant them now?

The principles involved in rooting plant parts (discussed earlier in this chapter) also apply to the germinating of seeds, with minor adaptation. A seed is an embryo plant stored in a shell and surrounded by a limited food supply. The length of time a seed will remain viable prior to sowing depends on the individual species plus the conditions under which it is stored. Most seeds store best at about 20°C but the critical prerequisite is a relative humidity of twenty per cent or lower. The latest techniques for lengthening the viability of ornamental seeds involve drying and sealing them in moisture-proof aluminum foil. The moisture a seed can pick up from being kept in humidity higher than twenty per cent will not be enough to germinate it but can be sufficient to abort the embryo seedling without any outward evidence that this has occurred. Storing seeds in airtight containers sealed under dry air conditions will extend the viability of the seed. So the seeds you have discovered may or may not be viable. The only certain test is to sow them correctly. In two to three weeks you will have the answer.

The best readily available media I have found for germinating seeds is the coarse peat-lite mix discussed in Chapter 1. Choose a container of a size appropriate to the number of seeds you are sowing, allowing each seed two square centimetres. Moisten the peat-lite in a dishpan by adding water and mixing. Peat-lite is often difficult to thoroughly moisten in the very dry packaged state and some stirring is usually necessary to accomplish this. However, do not overmix. The vermiculite particles break down rapidly during mixing in the presence of moisture and the necessary porous structure can be destroyed. Level the peat-lite in the container but do not pack (see Chapter 1 re stacking containers to improve drainage). Any seed the size of celery seed or smaller should not be covered or inadvertently buried by a post-seeding watering. Seeds the size of mustard or larger should be covered to no more than twice their thickness.

Watering

Just prior to sowing, thoroughly moisten the seed bed surface with a mister and then sow the seeds, spacing them as evenly as possible. With finer seed, pick up a pinch of seed between your thumb and forefinger and disburse them by slowly grinding these two fingers. Putting seeds in a V-shaped trough of stiff paper and then tapping the trough also works well. Very fine seeds such as Begonia seeds can be mixed with dry sand to give bulk and sown by either of the above methods. Cover with a clear plastic sheet, keeping the sheet about 2 cm above the surface. As in rooting plant parts, the plastic maintains high humidity, minimizes the need for watering and prevents drafts from drying out the seed bed. It also reduces evaporation from the seed bed surface which can lower the temperature as much as 2° to 4°C, to the detriment of seed germination. During the normal one to two week germinating period, no further watering should be required provided the sheet is secured so that drafts cannot reach the seed bed. The seed is very vulnerable at this point. Moisture activates the plant embryo within the seed. A drying out of the embryo or the emerging root and shoot will almost certainly have fatal results. Any application of water necessary to maintain moisture must be applied in the form of fine mist. Coarse spray can carry small seeds down into soil crevasses and bury them.

Temperature

For most house-plant seeds, the best germinating temperature is 26° to 28°C. Check the temperature by putting a thermometer on the seed bed. If you are using a fluorescent lighting unit, heat can be obtained by adding incandescent fixtures and bulbs. The red rays of the incandescent bulb's light spectrum will penetrate the plastic film and raise the media temperature. Monitor the temperature carefully and change the wattage of the bulbs to get desired results. Hot-water radiators are also a good source of heat under seedling containers. Control can be obtained by varying the height above the radiator, though remember that most radiators are under windows, which might put the seedling containers in direct sunlight. Use sheers to prevent direct sunlight on the seedbed when the plastic sheet is in place, otherwise the temperature under the plastic will skyrocket.

Light

Most seeds germinate best in the presence of light for at least twelve hours a day and preferably eighteen. Almost all benefit from continuous light, making lighting units (250 foot candles) ideal. With natural light, bright diffused light close to but not in direct sunlight is ideal. The plastic sheet should be removed as soon as the first leaves appear. If germination of the seeds is not uniform, the plastic must be removed when the most advanced seedlings reach 1 to 2 cm. Careful misting will then be necessary to maintain moisture around the seeds still in the process of germinating. Once the first set of true leaves appears on the most advanced seedlings, misting should be

114

discontinued on those plants and watering should be done, with a nozzle that will not beat down the young seedlings, whenever the soil surface feels dry. Misting after the first set of true leaves has appeared will result in soft growth that will go into shock when transplanted.

Transplanting

Transplanting involves digging out the seedlings (a table fork works well), and separating them into individual plants. Most of the germinating media will fall away from the roots and some of the root system will be lost in this operation. Transplant seedlings into individual pots or spaced out in a tray 5 to 10 cm apart. As with a new cutting, prevent severe wilting by frequent misting for the first few days after transplanting and avoid direct sunlight until the seedling is established. This should not take more than a week if a good, porous potting soil is used.

Avocado

I am fascinated with the idea of growing an Avocado plant from the pit. How do I go about it?

First eat the Avocado. They are delicious. With the flesh gone you now have a brown-skinned pit about the size of a golf ball. With a sharp knife or razor blade remove the top quarter of the seed. Then suspend the pit in water. The water should reach to within 1 cm of the top of the pit.

I have one of those bulb-forcing glasses that are used for Hyacinths. Would this work for the Avocado?

Yes, that would be fine. There are also glasses that are the shape of the old Coke glasses, narrow at the bottom and broadening out at the top. Often the bottom portion is the exact size required to suspend an Avocado in water. If neither of these is available you can insert toothpicks in the pit, Sputnik-style, and suspend the pit over a glass of water. Germination is very irregular and may take anywhere from a few days to a few months. When the pit has both stem and roots you can transfer it into soil. Use an open potting soil, just covering the top of the pit. Germination can take place in either dark or light but certainly once it does germinate it should be transferred to the light, and the more light the better.

Do I just let it grow after this?

Avocado plants are very unpredictable as to size and shape, but as a beginning rule, when the stem reaches a height of 15 cm, cut half of it off. This should cause branching.

One of the cleverest marketing coups of our day has been achieved by the producers of Avocados. They have convinced multitudes of people that an unedible pit one-third the size of the fruit is a very desirable state of affairs. Indeed, often the pit, not the edible part of the fruit, motivates the purchase.

In some cases when you cut open an Avocado you will find that the seed has already started to germinate. If this is the case do not, of course, cut off the top quarter of the seed. This operation is simply to aid germination in those seeds that have not started. Germination can be further speeded up and the vigour of the ensuing plant increased by storing the seed in the vegetable compartment of your refrigerator for four to six weeks. Before storing, clean the seed carefully under tepid water and then wrap it in moist, but not wet, paper towelling. Put it in a plastic bag and store it in the vegetable compartment of the refrigerator. This causes what plant physiologists call stratification. Care should be taken not to let the seed dry out. The seed may be safely stored in this manner for three to four months.

Instead of using water the seed can be started just as successfully by placing it in potting soil to a depth where the potting soil just covers the tip of the bulb. Water it thoroughly and wait for germination, keeping the soil constantly moist. The only real point in germinating the seed in water is to be able to see the rooting phenomenon.

Avocados grown from seed have very erratic growth habits. There is no way of predicting how the plant will grow or what shape it will be. Some send up a straight stem and others branch out at a very early stage While the pinching or topping operation described above sometimes works, it may also have little permanent effect. The plant may simply send out one branch which again heads straight up.

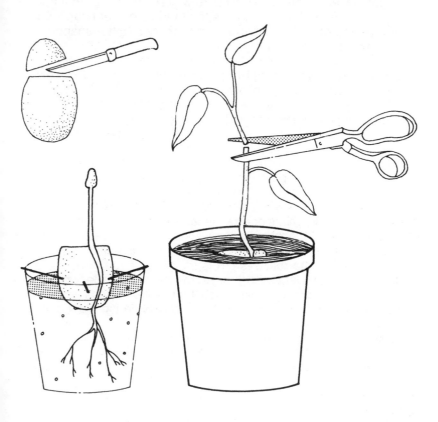

Removal of the top of the Avocado pit will expedite sprouting if the sprout is not already apparent. Toothpicks can be used to suspend the pit in water. Pinching is usually necessary to cause branching.

Another way to cause the plant to branch out is to split the upper-most tip of the plant to a depth of 5 to 10 cm. The plant may react to this by dying back along the split portion but usually two or three branches lower down are the result. The topping or splitting operation may take place on any of the subsequent branches whenever they get to the point where you would like to see them branch out. If you are successful in growing your Avocado you must also be bold in pruning it. If you don't, instead of having a tree that has a home life of five to six years, you will have an ugly specimen with wayward branches out-growing its space in three years or so.

If the one that you have germinated turns out to be an ugly tele-phone pole despite your best husbandry, all you can do is discard it and start several more. The only sure way of arriving at an attractive house plant using Avocado pits is to start lots of them continuously over a period of time, selecting from these the better-shaped ones and throwing the others away.

Avocados will grow well at room temperature and prefer full sun. Right in an east, west or south window in the winter is almost essen-tial. Watering and fertilizing practices mentioned in other places in this book apply equally to the Avocado plant. Keep in mind that an Avocado, in its native tropical habitat, gets a cool period of a month or two in its yearly cycle. This semi-dormant period seems to invigorate the tree and new growth follows. It would be desirable in April and May, or in the early fall, to expose the plant to the cooler outdoor climate, but not to the point where it receives frost.

Low light in the winter and low humidity may cause browning on the foliage. If the root system is healthy and the plant is growing and if there are no spider mites or other insects and the humidity is at forty per cent or above, then the plant is just having trouble adapting to the indoor environment. You may have to put up with a few brown spots on the foliage. If the root system is sound and you have not over-watered, but the plant develops some yellow foliage which later drops, then you can be almost certain that the light intensity is too low. Increase the light with artificial light or by moving the plant closer to the light source.

Avocados will benefit from a summer vacation outdoors in a shady spot. Care should be taken that you do not bring spider mites or other soil-borne insects in with the plant at the end of its summer holiday.

Best Methods of Propagation

The following lists classify house plants according to the best methods of propagation. Where a secondary and tertiary method may be used this is also noted by the appropriate abbreviation after the plant's name on the primary listing.

TC=terminal cutting (includes growing tip plus two to four mature leaves)
SC=stem cutting
RD=root division
SS=side shoots
AL=air layering
SL=soil layering
L=leaf propagation
VL=viviparous leaf propagation
LP=leaf petiole
S=seed or spore

Terminal and Stem Cuttings

ABUTILON
Flowering Maple

ACHIMENES (RT,S)
Magic Flowers

AESCHYNANTHUS
e.g. Lipstick Plant

APHELANDRA squarrosa
Zebra Plant

ARDISIA crenata (AL,S)
Coralberry

AZALEA

BEGONIA fibrous (S)

BEGONIA rieger
Aphrodite

BOUGAINVILLEA (SL)
Paper Flower

BUXUS
Boxwood

CITRUS
e.g. Calamondin Orange

CODIAEUM (AL)
Croton

COLUMNEA (RD)
e.g. Goldfish plant

CRASSULA (VL)
e.g. Jade Plant

DIPLADENIA (SL)

DRACAENA (AL)
e.g. Dragon Tree

EPISCIA (SL)
Flame Violets

EPIPREMNUM (SL)
Pothos

EUONYMUS
Spindle Tree

EUPHORBIA
e.g. Candelabra

FITTONIA (SL)
Nerve Plant

FUCHSIA

GARDENIA
Cape Jasmine

GERANIUM

GIBASIS (SL)
Tahitian Bridal Veil

GRAPTOPETALUM
Ghost Plant

GYNURA (SL)
Velvet Plant

HEDERA (SL)
Ivy

HIBISCUS (AL)
Mallow Rose

HOYA (SL)
Wax Vine

HYPOESTES
Polka-dot Plant

IMPATIENS
New Guinea

IRESINE
e.g. Bloodleaf

KALANCHOE (LP)
e.g. Velvet Leaf

MIKANIA
Plush Vine

MONSTERA (AL, S)
Cut-leaf Philodendron

NEMATANTHUS
e.g. Goldfish Plant

NERIUM (AL)
Oleander

PASSIFLORA (SL)
Passion Flower

PEPEROMIA (LP)
e.g. Glabella

PHILODENDRON (SL, AL)
e.g. Heartleaf Philodendron

PILEA
e.g. Aluminum Plant

PILEA depressa (SL)
Miniature Peperomia

PISONIA (AL)

PITTOSPORUM

PLECTRANTHUS (SL)
Swedish Ivy

PODOCARPUS (S)
e.g. Southern Yew

POLYSCIAS
e.g. Ming Aralia

PORTULACARIA
Elephant Bush

RHIPSALIDOPSIS
e.g. Easter Cactus

RUELLIA
Monkey Plant

SCHLUMBERGERA bridgesei
Christmas Cactus

SEDUM
e.g. Golden Glow

SENECIO (SL)
e.g. Wax Ivy

STENANDRIUM

SYNGONIUM (SL)
Nephthytis

TRADESCANTIA (SL)
Inch Plant

YUCCA elephantipes (SS)

ZEBRINA (SL)
Wandering Jew

Root Division

ANTHURIUM (TC)

AGLAONEMA (TC, S)
e.g. Chinese Evergreen

ASPIDISTRA
Cast Iron Plant

CALATHEA
e.g. Peacock Plant

CLIVIA (S)
Kafir Lily

MARANTA
Prayer Plant

POLYSTICHUM (S)
e.g. Holly Fern

SELAGINELLA
Cushion Moss

SOLEIROLIA
Baby's Tears

SPATHIPHYLLUM (S)
Peace Lily

Side Shoots

ALOE
e.g. Medicine Plant

ANANAS (TC)
Pineapple

BILLBERGIA
Queen's Tears

CRYPTANTHUS
Earthstars

CYCAS
Sago Palm

GUZMANIA

HAWORTHIA (LC, S)
e.g. Zebra Plant

HIPPEASTRUM
Amaryllis

NEOREGELIA
e.g. Blushing Bromeliad

NIDULARIUM

PANDANUS
Screw Pine

PLATACERIUM
Staghorn Ferns

SANSEVIERIA (VL)
Snake Plant

TILLANDSIA

VRIESEA (S)
e.g. Flaming Sword

Air Layering

COCCOLOBA
Sea Grape

CORDYLINE (TC)
e.g. Ti Plant

DIEFFENBACHIA (SS, SC)
Dumbcane

DIZYGOTHECA (S)
False Aralia

FATSHEDERA (SC)
Ivy Tree

FATSIA (TC)
Japanese Aralia

FICUS (SC)
e.g. Rubber Plant

Soil Layering

CHLOROPHYTUM comosum
Spider Plant

NEPHROLEPIS (RD)
e.g. Boston Fern

SAXIFRAGA sarmentosa
Strawberry Begonia

CISSUS (TC, SC)
e.g. Grape Ivy

Leaf Propagation

BEGONIA rex cultorum (AL)
Painted Leaf Begonia

TOLMIEA menziesii
Piggyback Plant

SEDUM morganianum (TC)
Burro's Tail

Viviparous Leaf Propagation

KALANCHOE daigremontiana X
tubiflora
Mother of Thousands

KALANCHOE gastonis-bonnieri
Good Luck Plant

Leaf Petiole

BEGONIA rieger
Schwabenland

GLOXINIA

SAINTPAULIA
African Violet

Seed and Spore Germination

ALSOPHILA cooperi
Australian Treefern

ARAUCARIA (AL)
e.g. Norfolk Island Pine

ASPARAGUS densiflorus (RD)
e.g. Sprengeri

ASPLENIUM nidus (VL)
Bird's Nest Fern

BEAUCARNEA recurvata
Ponytail Palm

BRASSAIA (AL)
Schefflera

CHAMAEDOREA (RD)
e.g. Bamboo Palm

CHRYSALIDOCARPUS
lutescens
Areca Palm

CYRTOMIUM falcatum (RD)
Holly Fern

FENESTRARIA aurantiaca
Baby's Toes

GLOXINIA (LP)

HOWEIA fosteriana
Kentia Palm

IMPATIENS
e.g. Elfin

LITHOPS
Living Stones

LIVISTONA chinensis
Chinese Fan Palm

PELLAEA (RD)
Cliffbrake Fern

PHOENIX
Date Palm

PTERIS
Table Ferns

SINNINGIA (LP)
Dwarf Gloxinia

STRETLITZIA reginae (RD)
Bird-of-Paradise

ZAMIA furfuracea
Jamaica Sago Tree

Chapter 9
Special Plants:
Cacti
Terrariums
Poisonous Plants: A Selected List

Ending your Cactus' Summer Vacation Outdoors

I have some medium-sized Cacti that I put out in their pots all summer. They have grown nicely and look very good. Do I have to do anything special before I bring them back into the house?

Have they been growing in full sunlight?

Yes, but I have gradually moved them to the point where they are now in shade.

You have the right technique. This helps them to acclimatize to the lower light in the home. If they have been sitting in soil while outside, or near flowerbeds, you might import some soil-borne insects into the home along with your Cactus. To be safe, dust the soil around the Cactus with 5% chlordane dust or 5% diazinon granules according to the directions on the container and water in the chemical thoroughly. A thorough drenching using malathion at the concentration recommended for spraying ornamentals has also been reported to be effective against wire worms and centipedes. I would do this a couple of weeks before bringing the plants into the house to make sure that you have the insects under control. At the same time I would suggest that you move the pots onto a patio or concrete walk where the Cacti will not be reinfested.

How late can I leave the Cacti outdoors?

This depends on the type of Cactus involved. If there are no Christmas or Orchid Cacti, which require a somewhat different treatment, then the ones you have will benefit from the lower temperatures that we get in the fall. The only thing you will have to watch is that you don't allow them to experience a hard frost. They can acclimatize to minor frosts and generally the lower temperatures in September are good for them. So listen to the weather forecast, and if a heavy frost is predicted, either cover them or bring them in.

Getting Your Cactus to Flower

I have a number of small Cacti, and I would love to get them to flower. I know they have to have a lower temperature and go into a dormant period first. I have one of them in a room which faces north. It gets very cool in the winter. Would it hurt to put all of them in there for the winter?

No. I think they will survive this but it would be better if they could be put in a room where they would get direct sunlight. If this is not possible, then the room facing north would likely work if they were really as close to the light as possible. The lower temperature is excellent treatment. Bear in mind that you will also have to cut down on the frequency of watering because you have reduced the growth rate due to lower temperatures and less light.

With the exception of the Christmas Cactus (Zygo cactus) and the Orchid Cactus (Epiphyllum cactus) a cold, dry treatment during the winter months benefits Cacti and duplicates the conditions that they would receive in their native habitat. Cacti grow naturally where there is no winter, and it is generally the rainless season that ends the active growth, completes the ripening of the wood and causes flowering. To induce budset under home conditions, it is necessary to lower temperature to about 5°C, and even down to freezing. Withhold water and give the plant plenty of light. These are not always easy conditions to provide. Certainly the plant will grow and survive with higher temperatures and more watering but it is difficult or impossible to get it to set buds and flower without duplicating these almost desert conditions.

To induce the Lovivia and Revutia varieties to bloom they must be kept almost bone dry from October through to January with maybe only one watering through all that period. This ought to cause wilting, which takes the form of softening and wrinkling of the surface as the cell structure shrinks without water. At the end of this period they should develop buds and flowers.

To help you identify a particular Cactus, there is a book called *Exotic Plant Manual* by A.B. Graff (Roehrs Company, East Rutherford, New Jersey, 07073). This is a pictorial dictionary of thousands of house plants with some cultural information, which should help you to ascertain the climatic conditions that you want to duplicate to encourage flowering. Apart from the Lovivia and the Revutia however, it is usually wise to lower the temperature to below 10°C and provide lots of light. In the winter months, do not water unless severe shrivelling takes place.

Care of a Christmas Cactus

How do I get my Christmas Cactus to bloom?

Essentially you must duplicate the conditions it would receive in its native habitat. This is done by withholding water, beginning in late August, to the point of minor wilting. Wilting can be detected by feeling the texture of the "leaves"; they will get softer as you withhold water. Water thoroughly only when they have become quite limp. Do not fertilize during this period of eight to twelve weeks. Place the plant where it will receive an average lower temperature down to 10°C, at least during the night hours. At the same time, you should begin to manipulate the day length, for the Christmas Cactus is photoperiodic and thermoperiodic. This means that it blooms in response to day length and temperature change. They should receive thirteen to fourteen hours of darkness and then full light for the other part of the day in addition to the cool, dry treatment. When the buds have set they can gradually be restored to room temperature and the normal day length.

What are the light requirements of the Christmas Cactus?

For the months of October through March it should be in a bright sunny window. In the summer the plant should be brought back further into the room because bright sunlight may cause burning of the plant tissue.

The purpose of withholding water during the changeover to the reproductive period (flowering and seed setting) on plants such as the Christmas Cactus is to ripen the wood and help the plant become reproductive. Any soft, lush-growing plant is always more difficult to bring into bloom. However, both lower temperatures (between 10° and 20°C) and a shortened day length (no longer than eleven hours) are also essential for budset.

The dropping of buds or flowers can be caused by a sudden drop of temperature or a change in the direction of light. It may also simply mean that the plant has set more buds than the light intensity can support. During the months of November through February move the plant as close to the window as possible or supplement normal light with artificial light. Day length must be controlled during the months of September, October and into November to a maximum of eleven hours, during which the plant must receive full light. The light energy promotes needed growth; the correct light duration and temperature determine budset. The thirteen-hour dark period must be continuous. Back in the forties when we were learning to time the maturity of Chrysanthemums by manipulating day length, it was said that if the greenhouse night watchman lit a match each night to check the thermometer the crop was delayed.

When the buds are plainly visible the light intensity becomes the critical issue. Even if the plant receives artificial light beyond eleven hours it will probably not delay its blooming. However, if it does not receive enough light intensity during this period it will probably have an effect on the quality or number of the blooms.

Once the flowering period has finished and the flowers have died, resume normal watering practices. Check the root system to make sure that the fertility content in the soil is not too high (see Chapter 3). If in doubt leach it. Once the plant starts growing (this should begin as the days get brighter and the light intensity increases in March and April) you could begin to fertilize again.

If you have been really successful in promoting new growth, in April, May and even June you can propagate cuttings. Simply break off a portion of the plant using about two sections from the tip of each branch and insert the lower section into a very open potting soil to a depth of about 2 cm. Propagate it the same way as you would do other cuttings (see Chapter 8). You can use a pot of about 7 cm in diameter for this operation or you can stick more than one cutting in a 12 cm pot and have an attractive multiple plant. Taking cuttings for new plants will also cause branching on the parent plant, bringing it into a more desirable shape.

Terrarium Plants: Watering Needs

We have a plant in one of those glass candy jars. We got it as a gift some three months ago and the plants were lovely and green. Now they are drying up.

The plants are planted down in the jar?

That's right.

How often have you watered it since you received it?

About once a week.

Can you actually see the soil?

Not really too well. It has those brown bark chips on the surface of the soil.

As the soil dries out it becomes much lighter brown in colour. When watered, it turns dark brown or black. Because you cannot feel the soil in most terrariums it is essential to be able to see whether the soil has dried out. You must either be able to see through the glass or look down through the opening in the top. I cannot believe that a terrarium in the shape of a candy jar, with that small opening, would allow enough water to evaporate from the plants to require watering once a week. I strongly suspect that this frequent watering has flooded the soil. The plant roots are now in water or in a very saturated soil and the roots have rotted.

I keep the top of the jar off. Wouldn't this compensate?

Not really. If you visualize that plant sitting in the room without the jar, you can see that the environment would be vastly different than the high-humidity situation inside the jar. I suggest you move that bark away when you are checking for water so that you can actually see the soil change colour. It is probably overwatered now, so it might not need water for two or three months. The excess water will slowly evaporate and as this happens the soil will dry out and new roots will begin to form. When the plant resumes normal growth, simply trim off the leaves that have been adversely affected.

Terrariums were first made and used about 150 years ago to transport plant material found in the far corners of the earth back to England. Nathaniel Ward, a physician and botanist, discovered that if he planted a plant in a glass-enclosed environment it evaporated very little water. They could put the plants in a terrarium (then called a Wardian Case) and ship it on sailing vessels, which had journeys of up to a year, without the plant needing water.

Depending on the size of the ventilation opening, terrariums crea a tropical environment with very high humidity. The smaller th opening of the terrarium the closer the humidity inside will be to or hundred per cent. This can promote very soft growth and disease. there is a large opening, it will be closer to room humidity, which cou be as low as thirty or forty per cent.

Most house plants grow best at a relative humidity of seventy pe cent. It is normal to have some condensation on the inside of th glass, but once it is heavy enough to collect and run down, th terrarium should be ventilated. This is not possible with a sma necked bottle, where it is even more important not to overwater. Wi terrariums that have larger openings, plastic wrap can be used close the opening partially until some condensation appears.

In the high-humidity terrarium situation, very little water is trans pired or evaporated and the need of the plant and the soil for water greatly reduced. Plants may go for as long as a year without add tional water after they have been planted in moist soil. While reservoir of crushed stone or charcoal in the bottom of the terrariu may act as a reservoir, it will not correct overwatering. The water w still collect there if overdone, and it may build up to affect the ro system and eventually the visible part of the plant.

A problem sometimes encountered in terrariums is that the high humidity provides an ideal environment for the incubation of th fungus disease Botrytis (see Chapter 5). As a precaution, use th spray dilution strength of benomyl as a drench covering both plan and soil with each watering.

Terrariums are, however, an excellent environment for certa plants that simply will not grow in the low humidity of many home Adiantum (Maidenhair Fern) and Selaginella, a beautiful little Mos Fern, are typical examples. See page 133 for a list of plants suitab for terrariums.

Potting Techniques for Terrariums

I need some help to set up a terrarium in a brandy magnum that I have. It is about 20 cm tall and about 22 cm across. What sort of base do I put in it and how deep should the soil be?

The purpose of the base material in the terrarium is to act as a reservoir for water and therefore it should discourage rooting down into that base. If it promotes rooting and is subsequently flooded with drainage water, the roots will rot, which will show up later as damaged leaves. Horticultural charcoal (charcoal that has not been treated by an agent to increase its ability to burn) in pieces of 1 to 3 cm makes an ideal base material. In a terrarium the size that you are talking about you need a depth of 4 to 6 cm. Over this, spread 3 to 5 cm of potting soil.

Now what can I plant in it?

You are dealing with quite a small container, so the plants that you choose must be naturally dwarf growing or be readily pruned to keep them dwarf. You can use something taller in the centre which could eventually come up through the opening such as Neanthe Bella Palm. You could use Dwarf Fittonia which has nice green foliage with white veins. Selaginella or Moss Fern would be ideal in a small terrarium like this.

What about flowering plants?

Yes, you could use African Violets or Dwarf Gloxinia.

The choice of plant material for a terrarium depends on the size of the terrarium, the type of glass, the size of the opening, and whether or not that opening can be varied in size. These factors will also determine where the terrarium can be placed in terms of its exposure to light.

If it is a clear glass wine bottle with a very small opening and you place it in direct sunlight, it will trap heat to the point of destroying the plant material inside. A glass wine bottle with a green tint will filter out as much as fifty per cent of the light. This means that you may be able to place it in direct sunlight, particularly in the winter. It would be wise in any location to check that the temperature is not rising above 30°C (the point at which growth of most plants stops) by lowering a thermometer into the bottle.

If the opening is large and can be varied by putting something over it, then you can place the terrarium where it receives direct sunlight and ventilate through the opening as required. This allows for the planting of species requiring higher light, giving you a greater choice of plant material.

In larger terrariums it is advisable to increase the depth of the material used as a reservoir and the soil to about twenty per cent of the height. In choosing plants make sure that they are compatible in terms of their light requirements (see Chapter 4).

List of Plants for Terrariums

Plants are listed in order of those tolerating the lowest light to those requiring higher light.

F=Flowers intermittently or seasonally.

Growth Type indicates in what direction you may expect the plant to grow so that you can allocate space in relation to other plants.

V: Vertical growth habit
S: Spreading growth habit
VS: Mostly vertical growth with some spreading
SV: Mostly spreading with some vertical growth
GC: Prostrate ground cover type growth

Pruning indicates those plants which can be pruned (branches and/or terminal) to restrict growth.

Minimum indicates the smallest dimension (either height for vertical-growing plants or width for a spreading plant) of a terrarium practical for a single plant, assuming that you start with a plant growing in a 5 to 8 cm pot. The same dimension indicates the growth space required in a larger terrarium with other plant material on the basis of one year's growth. If the plant can be pruned the "minimum" figure is on the basis of judicial pruning. All of these figures are, of course, approximate only. Horticulture is not an exact science—at least not the way I practise it.

BOTANICAL AND COMMON NAME	GROWTH	PRUNE	MINIMUM
SANSEVIERIA trifasciata 'Hahnii' Bird's Nest Sansevieria	VS	No	12 cm
DRACAENA surculosa Gold Dust Dracaena	VS	Yes	10 cm
DRACAENA godseffiana Florida Beauty	VS	Yes	10 cm
PEPEROMIA sandersii Watermelon Peperomia	S	No	15 cm
PEPEROMIA orba Princess Astrid Peperomia	SV	Yes	15 cm

PEPEROMIA obtusifolia 'Variegata' Variegated Pepper Face	VS	Yes	15 cm
PEPEROMIA caperata Emerald Ripple Peperomia	S	No	12 cm
PEPEROMIA clusiifolia Red-edged Peperomia	VS	Yes	15 cm
CHAMAEDOREA elegans bella Neanthe Bella Palm	V	No	10 cm
DRACAENA sanderiana Ribbon Plant	V	Yes	12 cm
POLYSTICHUM tsus-simense Korean Holly Rockfern	VS	No	5 cm
NEPHROLEPIS exaltata Dwarf Fluffy Ruffles Fern	VS	No	5 cm
SELAGINELLA kraussiana 'Brownii' Cushion Moss Gold and Green	S	No	5 cm
SELAGINELLA martensii 'Watson-iana' Lycapodium Moss	S	No	5 cm
PELLAEA rotundifolia Cliffbrake Fern	S	No	10 cm
ADIANTUM fragrantissimum Maidenhair Fern	VS	No	10 cm
ADIANTUM hispidulum Australian Maidenhair Fern	VS	No	15 cm
ADIANTUM raddianum Pacific Maidenhair Fern	V	No	10 cm
PTERIS cretica 'albo-lineata' Variegated Table Fern	V	No	15 cm
PTERIS ensiformis 'Victoriae' Victoria Table Fern	V	No	15 cm
PTERIS cretica 'Wilsonii' Fan Table Fern	V	No	10 cm
SOLEIROLIA soleirolii Baby's Tears	GC	Yes	15 cm

STENANDRIUM lindenii	S	Yes	10 cm
DIEFFENBACHIA exotica Dwarf Dumbcane	V	No	25 cm
MARANTA leuconeura Prayer Plant	VS	Yes	15 cm
ANTHURIUM scherzerianum F Flamingo Plant	VS	No	30 cm
SYNGONIUM podophyllum Nephthytis Vine	VS	Yes	25 cm
CRYPTANTHUS bivittatus Earth Stars	S	No	15 cm
PILEA microphylla Artillery Plant	S	No	15 cm
PILEA cadierei Aluminum Plant	S	Yes	15 cm
PILEA involucrata Friendship Plant	S	Yes	15 cm
PILEA depressa Creeping Pilea	GC	Yes	15 cm
CRASSULA portulacea Crosby's Compacta	VS	Yes	20 cm
CRASSULA lycopodioides Watchchain Jade Plant	S	Yes	15 cm
CRASSULA tetragona Pine Tree Jade	VS	Yes	20 cm
MIKANIA ternata Plush Vine	GC	Yes	10 cm
FICUS pumila Creeping Fig	GC	Yes	15 cm
HAWORTHIA limifolia keithii	S	No	10 cm
CYRTOMIUM falcatum Holly Fern	SV	No	20 cm
APHELANDRA squarrosa F Zebra Plant	V	Yes	20 cm

CORDYLINE terminalis Baby Ti	V	Yes	15 cm
ARAUCARIA heterophylla Norfolk Island Pine	V	No	20 cm
BILLBERGIA (many species) F e.g. Queen's Tears	V	No	20 cm
VRIESEA splendens Painted Feathers	VS	No	15 cm
TILLANDSIA (many species) e.g. Silver Birds	VS	No	15 cm
PITTOSPORUM tobira Mock Orange	VS	Yes	15 cm
GRAPTOPETALUM paraguayense Ghost Plant	S	No	10 cm
EUONYMUS japonicus Goldspot and others	V	Yes	15 cm
ARDISIA crispa Coral Berry	SV	Yes	15 cm
IRESINE (many species) e.g. Bloodleaf	V	Yes	20 cm
ASPARAGUS densiflorus 'Meyersii' Foxtail Fern	VS	No	20 cm
CRASSULA anomala Dwarf Jade Plant	SV	Yes	15 cm
KALANCHOE beharensis Felt Plant	VS	Yes	15 cm
KALANCHOE tomentosa Panda Plant	VS	Yes	15 cm
PORTULACARIA afra African Jade	VS	Yes	15 cm
FENESTRARIA rhopalophylla Baby's Toes	S	No	3 cm
CODIAEUM punctatum aureum Gold Dust Croton	VS	Yes	20 cm

SAINTPAULIA ionantha F African Violet	S	No	15 cm
SINNINGIA speciosa F Dwarf Gloxinia	S	No	5 cm
HYPOCYRTA (many species) F e.g. Goldfish Plant	GC	No	20 cm
AESCHYNANTHUS (many species) F upright types	GC	No	20 cm
EPISCIAS (many species) F Flaming Violet	GC	Yes	25 cm
DIZYGOTHECA elegantissima False Aralia	V	No	15 cm
PODOCARPUS macrophyllus Southern Yew	VS	Yes	15 cm
ALOE variegata Tiger Aloe	VS	No	10 cm

Botanical and common names are taken from the 1977 edition of *Hortus Third*.

Poisonous Plants: A Selected List

Is there any truth to recent articles that say that cultivated and natural plants are poisonous?

Yes, there is. Some of the plants are sold in plant shops, greenhouses and nurseries.

I keep hearing stories about Poinsettias being poisonous. Has anyone died from eating a Poinsettia?

No. There isn't a single documented case. In December, 1975, the U.S. Consumer Products Safety Commission declared that the Poinsettia should not be classified as a poisonous plant or as a serious risk in the home. A child would have to eat more than a pound of the plant before getting sick. Considering the bitter taste of the Poinsettia, even a young child wouldn't do that.

Has anyone died from eating any plants?

Yes, but there are no reliable statistics available on the number of persons fatally poisoned by plants. Keep in mind that poisonous isn't always synonymous with death. The vast majority of persons alleged to have ingested a poisonous plant experience only minor upset or distress. Experts agree that there are hundreds of poisonous plants, most of them growing wild. Dr. Julia Morton, Research Associate and Director of Morton Collectanea at the University of Miami, says in her book, *Plants Poisonous to People*, that the principal hazard is that people are unfamiliar with the properties of plants. For example, she noted that tuber sprouts of the ordinary potato can be poisonous when ingested.

Isn't it difficult to stop children from eating plants?

Of course. As Dr. Morton says in her book, children must be regarded as "grazing animals." Pets are less of a concern. One serious problem I am aware of with animals is if the plant material they could normally ingest has been poisoned by a chemical such as Paraquat, a herbicide used on weeds or grass.

Eating the wrong kind of fruit has bedevilled mankind ever since the Garden of Eden. The fact that we not only still exist but have multiplied greatly indicates that we have learned through one experience or another the plants that are to be avoided. Ornamental and wild plants are usually not edible.

The number of plant poisonings is comparatively small considering the number of times children and adults are exposed to plants. Plants known to have toxic properties should be treated with the same respect given to household hazards such as matches, electricity, gasoline, insecticides and the contents of the medicine cabinet. This list of poisonous plants is not all-inclusive but it does suggest some of the common cultivated and wild plants which have been shown to be poisonous. When in doubt, do not eat plants. Consider them poisonous.

If plant poisoning does occur in spite of all precautions, the usual treatment is to empty the stomach as quickly as possible, either mechanically—with a finger in the throat—or with a non-prescription drug called Ipecac. The next step is to rush the victim to the doctor or the hospital. The drug Ipecac is available in most drug stores in doses premeasured for children. It would be a good item to include in any first-aid kit.

Azalea (entire plant): Paralysis of the muscles, including the heart; depression of the central nervous system. Sometimes fatal.

Baneberry, *Actaea* spp. (all parts, especially the roots and berries): Severe stomach cramps, increased pulse, delirium, dizziness, and circulatory failure. White or red berries on swollen red stalks are very attractive to children. As few as six berries can cause severe symptoms.

Belladona, *Atropa belladonna* (fruit): Ingestion of three berries has been known to be fatal to a child.

Bird-of-Paradise, *Strelitzia reginae* (seed pods): Nausea, vomiting and diarrhea.

Black Locust, *Robinia pseudoacacia* (bark, foliage, young sprouts): Depression, vomiting, diarrhea and weakened heartbeat. Often fatal.

Boxwood, *Buxus sempervirens* (foliage): May cause dermatitis in some people. In Maryland, a report of sheep mortality from hedge clippings has been made.

Calla Lily, *Lantedeschia aethiopica* (entire plant): Intense burning sensation and irritation of the mouth and stomach.

Castor Bean, *Ricinnus communis* (entire plant but especially seeds): Burning sensation in mouth. Swallowing two or more seeds may cause serious illness.

Wild and Cultivated Cherries and Choke Cherries, *Prunus* spp. (all parts except fruit, particularly bark, leaves and seeds; the fruit is edible if the seeds are removed): Toxic plant parts cause cyanide poisoning leading to difficult breathing, paralysis of the voice, coma of short duration and death. Toxic parts of related native and culti-

139

vated species of cherry, laurel cherry, plum, almond, and peach have similar effects. Excessive quantities of apple and crab apple seeds also produce cyanide poisoning.

Christmas Rose, *Helleborus niger* (entire plant): Common garden perennial long considered poisonous.

Clematis spp. (entire plant): All species contain some cyanide and may be dangerous.

Croton (sap): Formerly used in medicine as a purgative and one of the most drastic available. Only a few drops of the pure oil are lethal to animals.

Daffodil (bulb): Severe vomiting and diarrhea, trembling, convulsions and sometimes death.

Daphne (entire plant): Burning and ulceration of stomach and intestines, bloody vomiting and diarrhea.

Deadly or Bittersweet Nightshade, Black Nightshade, Horse Nettle, *Solanum* spp. (all parts, especially unripe berries): Stomach pain, dilated pupils, circulatory and respiratory depression, vomiting, diarrhea, paralysis, loss of sensation, and death. People have many confusing ideas about the poisonous qualities of this plant because of the harmless nature of the completely ripe fruit of a few species.

Dumbcane, *Dieffenbachia* spp. (entire plant): Biting, chewing or tasting this plant rapidly produces irritation and burning of the mouth, tongue and lips. Copious salivation and swelling which may make the tongue immobile.

English Ivy, *Hedera helix* (leaves, fruit): A few cases of poisoning after ingestion of the berries have been reported.

Euonymus spp. (leaves, bark, fruit): Cases of violent purgation in horses and poisoning in humans have been described in Europe.

European Beech, *Fagus sylvatica* (seeds): Cases of poisoning in humans after ingestion of the seeds have been reported in Europe.

Foxglove, *Digitalis purpurea* (entire plant): Contains chemicals which stimulate the heart. Poisoning in humans results from overdoses of these chemicals.

Holly, *Illix* spp. (berries): Vomiting, diarrhea, weakness and collapse.

Horse Chestnut, *Aesculus hippocastanum* (fruit, leaves): In Europe it has been stated that ingestion of the nuts has killed children.

Iris (leaves, roots and fleshy portion): Severe but temporary digestive upset.

Jack-in-the-Pulpit, *Arisaema* spp. (entire plant): Needle-like crystals of calcium oxalate are present, particularly in the rhizome. These crystals may become embedded in the mucous membranes of the mouth and provoke intense irritation.

Jerusalem Cherry, *Solanum* spp. (leaves, fruit): It is safest to consider any species potentially poisonous until determined otherwise. Toxicity is not lost in drying.

Jimsonweed, *Datura* (all parts, especially the seeds and leaves): Intense thirst, pupil dilation, redness of skin, dryness of mouth, hallucinations, rapid pulse, convulsions, coma and death. Children have been poisoned by sucking nectar from the flowers, eating the seeds, or making "tea" from the leaves. Only a small amount of seeds can be fatal.

Kentucky Coffee Tree, *Gynmocladus dioica* (fruit, leaves, sprouts): A case has been reported where a woman was poisoned when she mistook this tree for a honey locust and ate some fruit pulp from it.

Lantana (leaves, fruit): Lantana poisoning has been reported fatal in children.

Larkspur, *Delphinium* (entire plant): All species, even the ones commonly cultivated in flower gardens, should be considered potentially toxic.

Lily-of-the-Valley, *Convallaria majalis* (entire plant): Lily-of-the-Valley has long been considered a poisonous plant.

Mayapple, Mandrake, *Podophyllum peltatum* (all parts, except edible ripe fruit): Severe stomach upset, vomiting. Children have been poisoned by eating too much unripe fruit. May also cause dermatitis.

Milkweed, *Asclepias* spp. (entire plant): It is likely that many or all species have some degree of toxicity.

Mistletoe, *Phoradendron* and *Viscum* spp. (white berries): Can cause severe stomach and intestinal irritation with diarrhea and slow pulse. Several deaths among children have been attributed to eating the berries. Tea brewed from the berries has caused fatality.

Oleander, *Nerium* (entire plant): Cultivated widely throughout the U.S. Widespread fatalities in some countries.

Philodendron, spp. (entire plant): Same as those of Dieffenbachia but less severe. Monstera (Cut-leaf Philodendron), Anthurium, Colocasia (Elephant Ears), Caladium and other members of the Arum family have similar effects. Cats are especially susceptible to Philodendron poisoning.

Poison Ivy, *Rhus radicans*/**Poison Sumac,** *Rhus vernix* (entire plant): Inflammation and swelling accompanied by intense irritation and followed by formation of blisters. Careful washing of exposed parts soon after contact will remove excess resin. An alkali soap is best since the resin is soluble in oils present in many soaps. This helps to keep from rubbing resin on other parts of the body. The resin is readily carried by particles in smoke when burned and remains effective for years. It is also spread by pets who have been in contact with the plants. Poison Sumacs are distinguished from other non-toxic Sumacs by their clusters of white to yellow fruit along the branches.

Potato, Irish Potato, White Potato, *Solanum tuberosum* (green "sunburned" spots and sprouts of potato tubers, stems, leaves and fruit): Stomach pain, cold and clammy skin, nausea, mental confusion and respiratory and cardiac depression. Tomato plants (except the edible fruit) and Tobacco plants have similar effects.

Privet, *Ligustrum* spp. (entire plant): Bloody vomiting, diarrhea, severe irritation of digestive tract and general nervous system.

Ragweed, *Ambrosia artemisiifolia* (pollen): This and other ragweeds produce large quantities of windborne pollen which is responsible for about ninety per cent of the cases of late summer and fall hayfever.

Ranunculus or Buttercup (entire plant): Stomach irritation, diarrhea and, in large quantities, convulsions.

Rhodendron spp. (entire plant): Watering of mouth, eyes, and nose. Slow pulse, vomiting, low blood pressure, convulsions, lack of coordination and progressive paralysis of arms and legs until death. Children have been poisoned by sucking on the flowers and by making "tea" from the leaves.

Rhubarb, *Rheum rhaponticum* (leaf blade; not the leaf stalk or petiole which is edible): Stomach pains, nausea, difficulty in breathing, burning of mouth and throat, internal bleeding and coma. Death or permanent kidney damage can occur without treatment. Hogs and other animals have been killed when fed the leaves.

Rosary Pea, Jequirity Bean, Precatory Bean, Crabs-eye, Prayer Bean, *Abrus precatorius* (seeds): Severe stomach irritation, incoordination and paralysis. Less than one seed is fatal if the seed coat has been broken. These colourful scarlet seeds with black tips have been used in necklaces, rosaries, etc. and the poison can be taken in through a pricked finger while stringing the beans.

Stinging Nettle, *Urtica* spp. (stinging hairs on stems and leaves): Intense itching usually of short duration. Has caused serious problems with hunting dogs characterized by excessive salivation, pawing at the mouth, respiratory distress, slow and irregular heartbeat, and muscular weakness.

Sweet Buckeye, *Aesculus octandra* (fruit, leaves): This species is considered one of the ten most troublesome poisonous plants, according to the Poisonous Plants Bulletin of the North Carolina Experimental Station.

Water Hemlock, Spotted Cowbane, *Cicuta maculata* (all parts, especially the roots): Violent convulsions, diarrhea, tremors, frothing at the mouth, delirium, dilated pupils, extreme stomach pain and death. Often mistaken for Wild Parsnip or Wild Artichoke. The roots are extremely poisonous, and one mouthful is sufficient to kill a grown man.

Wisteria (entire plant): Severe vomiting, abdominal pain and diarrhea.

Yew, Ground Hemlock, Japanese Yew, *Taxus* spp. (foliage, bark and seeds): Taxus baccata is considered the most dangerous of all poisonous trees and shrubs. Nausea, vomiting, diarrhea, abdominal pain, circulatory failure and difficulty in breathing. Can also cause dermatitis. Yew is used extensively around homes as foundation planting.

Glossary

anther: The pollen-bearing top of the stamen.

bract: A leaf of a plant growing around the flower or flower stem differing from other leaves in shape or colour.

budset: The time in the life cycle of flowering plants at which the flower bud is initiated.

canker: Part of the common name of some plant diseases (e.g. Rose Canker). The result of the death of a clearly defined area of the stem or leaf usually resulting in the corrosion and sloughing away of tissue and, finally, an open wound.

chlorophyll: The green colouring matter of leaves and plants, essential to the production of carbohydrates by photosynthesis.

compensation point: That point at which the food energy required by the plant during respiration is equal to the amount produced by photosynthesis. There is neither a net gain nor a net loss in growth.

contact insecticide: An insecticide that remains on the applied surface and is not absorbed into the plant tissue. It is effective in killing insects as long it is not washed away or broken down by the environment.

corm: A bulb-like subterranean stem, solid (unlike a bulb) and oval in shape (unlike a tuber).

cultivar: See **species.**

damping off: A disease of seedlings, occurring after they emerge from the soil, caused by certain soil fungi and resulting in wilting and collapse of the plant.

family: See **species.**

foot candle (FC): A foot candle is a unit of illumination, equivalent to the illumination produced by a source of one candle at a distance of one foot. Light intensity drops off at the rate of the square of the distance from the source. Two feet from a fluorescent tube, the light will be one quarter of the amount at the tube itself. This means that the leaves at the bottom of a six-foot high Schefflera will be getting a lot less light than those at the top. In SI *(Système internationale d'unités)* one foot candle equals 10.763 91 lux.

free moisture: Any moisture that is surplus to that which can be held on the soil particles by surface tension or absorbed by organic matter in the growing media.

fungicide: A chemical that kills fungus.

genus: (pl. genera) See **species.**

germination: The resumption of growth by any spore or seed after a period of dormancy.

guttation: The extrusion of water from the hydathodes of leaves under conditions of high water intake and low evaporation.

hydathodes: Permanently open microscopic structures of a leaf that allow the passage of water, usually occurring along the margins and tips of the leaves.

leaf axil sheath or stipule: Located where the leaf stem (petiole) joins the stem on some but not all plants. They vary greatly in form from species to species.

leaf blade: The broad part of a leaf excluding the petiole.

lesion: A clearly defined injured area of stem or leaf tissue caused by disease or physical injury.

peat-lite mix: A synthetic growing media consisting of sphagnum peat moss, vermiculite and/or perlite, chemical nutrients, limestone and no soil.

perlite: A form of volcanic rock that contains sodium and aluminum in amounts that can be extracted by growing plants. Perlite does not decay or deteriorate except through physical destruction. It holds water on its irregular surface areas.

petiole: The stem of a leaf.

pH: A measure of acidity or alkalinity (7.0 is neutral, below this is acid, above is alkaline). The pH factor affects the availability of nutrients to the plant.

photosynthesis: The process in which carbon dioxide and water in the presence of light and chlorophyll are converted into carbohydrates.

pinching: The removal of the growing tip or branches of a plant for the purpose of causing branching.

pistil: The female or seed-bearing organ of a flower consisting of ovary, style and stigma.

rhizome: A creeping, horizontal underground stem.

scarify: To scratch the surface of the root ball, loosening some or all of the surface roots.

species: (spp.) Within the scope of this book a **family** is the broadest classification of plants and is based on the resemblances in the structure of the flowers, especially of its reproductive organs, the stamens and pistil. It is agreed practice, however, for plant names to begin with the next major classification, **genus.** The next classification in the plant hierarchy is **species.** This is a kind of plant that retains its distinctiveness from other kinds over many generations. In commercial horticulture a further selection is made because of some distinctive merit or hybridization which is called a **cultivar** or **variety.** Thus Grape Ivy belongs to the Vitaceae family. Its botanical name is made up of its genus (Cissus) and its species (rhombifolia). One of its recent cultivars is 'Ellen Danica.'

spore: A reproductive body of lower plants that corresponds in function to a seed but possesses no embryo.

stamen: The male organ of the flower.

stem cutting: A portion of the stem of a plant usually including at least one leaf.

stigma: The part of the pistil which receives the pollen.

stratification: The physiological changes in a bulb that take place during dormancy and are necessary for flowering.

systemic insecticide: An insecticide that is absorbed into the tissue of a plant on application and translocated throughout the plant.

terminal growth: The uppermost growth tip of a plant.

transpiration: The evaporation and consequent loss of water from a living plant.

tuber: A thickened portion (as the potato) of an underground stem, bearing buds or "eyes" from which new plants may arise.

up-potting: To repot a plant into a larger container.

variety: See **species.**

vermiculite: Vermiculite contains some potassium and magnesium and has a unique structure which enables it to hold and release large quantities of water and minerals for plant growth.

Index

dimethoate 23%, 65, 70
endosulfon, 61, 68
ethion, 69
malathion, 61, 65, 66, 69, 70, 125
methoxychlor, 61
oxydemeton-methyl, 65, 68, 69, 70
primicarb, 68
resmethrin, 60, 68, 69
tetradefon, 69
Insects
aphids, 67-8
centipedes, 125
fungus gnats, 59-60
mealy bugs, 70
scale, 65-6
spider mites, 67, 68-9, 118
whiteflies, 61-2
wire worms, 125
Ipecac, 139
Iresine, 56, 68, 120, 135
Iris, 140
Iron, 36, 38
Ivy, 48, 52, 67, 69, 104, 120, 122

Jack-in-the-Pulpit, 141
Jade Plant, 29, 30, 50, 110, 119
Jamaica Sago Plant, 52, 123
Janet Craig, 50
Japanese Aralia, 56, 122
Japanese Yew, 143
Jequirity Bean, 142
Jerusalem Cherry, 141
Jimsonweed, 141

Kafir Lily, 57, 121
Kalanchoe, 108, 120
   beharensis, 136
   diagremontiana X tubiflora, 108, 122
   gastonis bonnieri, 108, 122
   tomentosa, 136
Kentia Palm, 50, 123
Kentucky Coffee Tree, 141
Kleinia gomphophylla, 56
Korean Rockfern, 51, 134

Lance Dracaena, 53
Lantana, 141
Lantedeschia aethiopica, 139
Larkspur, 141
Leaching, 29-30, 32, 34, 39, 80, 88, 108, 128
Leaf axil shield, 92
Leaf petiole propagation, 111-12, 122
Leaf propagation, 106-7, 122
Life Plant, 108
Light
   artificial, 39, 41-2, 49, 86, 87, 108, 114, 127, 128
   compensation point, 44
   fluorescent, 41, 114
   foot candle, 49-57, 89, 114
   grow lights, 41
   incandescent, 41, 114
   meter, 46, 49
Ligustrum, 142
Lily of the Valley, 141
Limestone, 16, 17, 36
Lipstick Plant, 45, 119
Lithops, 55, 57, 123
Living Stones, 55, 57, 123
Livistona chinensis, 50, 123
Lovivia, 126
Lycapodium Moss, 134

Magic Flowers, 119
Magnesium, 16, 36, 38
Maidenhair Fern, 51, 130, 134
Malathion, see Insecticides
Malaysian Dracaena, 53
Mallow Rose, 120
Mandrake, see Mayapple
Manganese, 36, 38
Manure, 34
Maranta, 25, 52, 70, 121
Mayapple, 141
Mealy bugs, see Insects
Medicine Plant, 121
Methoxychlor, see Insecticides
Mikania, 120
   ternata, 53, 135
Mildew, 47
Milkweed, 141
Mimosa pudica, 54